BLACK BOY POEMS

CURRICULUM

BY
TYSON AMIR

Black Boy Poems
Curriculum For Revolutionary Instruction
by
Tyson Amir
Freedom Soul Media

ISBN-10: 0-9977985-2-1

ISBN-13: 978-0-9977985-2-4

Cover design by Self-Publishing Services LLC (www.Self-Publishing-Service.com)

Edited by Freedom Soul Media

Formatted by Freedom Soul Media

May this work be a true way of honoring our elders who taught me with this philosophy in mind:

*"We Want Education For Our People That Exposes
The True Nature Of This Decadent Society.
We Want Education That Teaches Us Our True History
And Our Role In The Present-Day Society."*

- Black Panther Party 10 Point Platform and Program, Point 5

This work would not be possible without contributions from three very talented minds that helped move this project along. Ana Benderas, Nomsa Mabona and Alia Gabres. Thank you for your vision and passion. This is just the beginning. We have much more work to do.

Black Boy Poems Curriculum

Philosophy of Curriculum

Black Boy Poems is a revolutionary literary work that combines social/political commentary, historical and contemporary analysis with high levels of Hip Hop praxis. This accompanying curriculum allows instructors and learners to engage in a learning experience like none other. The Black Boy Poems Curriculum is necessary because too often the curricula in learning spaces are built in ways that do not engender critical thinking, enthusiasm and consistent and eager participation in our learners. One of the main reasons for this phenomena is the fact that those curricula are lacking cultural relevance and are devoid of methods and strategies that allow learners to position their varying social contexts/experiences in the learning space.

Our learning spaces are extremely diverse in terms of cultures, languages, ethnicities, learning levels/styles and backgrounds. With so much diversity it is incumbent upon us to find new ways of reaching our learners. A significant number of them excitedly and willingly participate in Hip Hop culture. The process of learning is heavily influenced by the culture(s) a learner possesses. This means that a pedagogy rooted in an authentic Hip Hop praxis firmly steeped in the context that produced and continues to produce Hip Hop has the potential to activate, inspire, empower and educate our learners.

Hip Hop pedagogy has become a popular buzzword in academia and education. However, Hip Hop is not a byproduct of either of those spaces, and has historically been shunned by those spaces. In order to arrive at an authentic Hip Hop pedagogy the creators of the culture must be the driving force behind how it's used in an educational setting. This forces the worlds of academia and education to abdicate their roles as shapers of the institutions and partner with those, and at times learn from those who have expertise in those areas.

Having a degree in teaching doesn't make one a "great" teacher. Having a mastery of the Hip Hop art form doesn't make one able to use Hip Hop as a teaching toll. What is needed is to find people who are competent in both areas. Those people must have a mastery of Hip Hop, and not just as a fan but as a practitioner; and a mastery of facilitating education in diverse learning spaces. My background as an educator, Hip Hop artist, poet, author and activist allows me to harness the best in these different disciplines and combine them in a focused and comprehensive way that promotes a quality culturally relevant learning experience.

Decolonizing Education

A major part of the learning philosophy in this curriculum is decolonization. Education can either help perpetuate colonization or it can be a catalyst for liberating hearts, minds and bodies. I've adopted an approach that is intentional about decolonizing the education process. Hence the use of specific terminology. The "work" that learners will complete is called a Learning Experience instead of a "lesson" or "assignment".

I personally believe the words "lesson" and "assignment" in the context of education in western society reflect a level of cultural arrogance on the part of the institution. The institution of education has largely been guided by people with no real knowledge of some of these diverse learning communities. These institutions hold the decision making power that determines what learners must learn. The process of constructing and facilitating learning should be more inclusive and cooperative. When inclusion and cooperation are not present the dynamic between institution and learner becomes authoritarian. "Lessons" and "assignments" are superimposed upon a population that has no choice in the matter. Learning Experience is a term that better represents the ideal of a collaborative process of learning that all will participate in.

I also use the term "Learner" instead of student. I believe the learning space is a place where everyone will learn. There is no hierarchy when it comes to learning. The "teacher" will learn and the "students" will learn. To reflect this idea more, I chose to refer to all members in the learning space as learners. I believe this helps define the space as a space where all of us will participate and learn. Each of us will play a role in facilitating the learning process.

Most importantly the process of education has to be focused on providing an educational experience that encourages learners to think about and work for freedom and liberation instead of conforming and assimilation. Our society is in desperate need of systemic change. Our education institution is complicit in contributing to the state of our world today because we are not preparing our learners for the world, or helping them to think about ways they can contribute to changes in our world.

Every metric we use to analyze the quality of education provided to black learners and other learners of color shows that we are failing them. This is coupled with what has been termed as the school-to-prison pipeline, where the clear correlation between failing educational systems and our learners (mainly black and brown) becoming incarcerated in jails and prisons (and at times far more worse fates) has been firmly established. This is a small snapshot of the context of public education today. In the face of these realities we are still attempting to employ curricula that do not connect with the learners we have in our learning spaces. They certainly do not inspire and empower them with a sense of self and an understanding of the revolutionary power they posses.

The Black Boy Poems Curriculum was not created to perpetuate the issues in education today. It was developed specifically with the goals of providing a revolutionary educational experience that equips learners with valuable skills, an understanding of self and encourages them to work for change in our society. Education is essential for individual growth and change. May we begin to work to provide an education that helps to produce learners who know themselves, know the world around them and contribute to changing our world for the better.

Structure of curriculum

There are 16 main chapters in Black Boy Poems. The curriculum is designed to explore each chapter individually. Every chapter has at least six different Learning Experiences. Five of those learning experiences will appear in every chapter (Common Learning Experiences). This helps to build a routine that the learners will become more familiar with as they progress through the text and curriculum. Every chapter also contains at least one Unique Learning Experience that is based on the content in the poem and the chapter. More Learning Experiences will be added to each chapter as the curriculum continues to evolve.

Learning Experiences

Every poem in the book has a video for the learners to watch so they can hear the poem directly from the author. Receiving the content directly from the creator of the material is culturally significant. After listening to and reading the poem the learners will be asked to work on the first Learning Experience, the Initial Poem Reflection.

The Learning Experiences are as follows:

- Initial Poem Reflection Learning Experience
- Vocabulary Learning Experience
- Second Poem Reflection Learning Experience
- Unique Learning Experience
- Deep Dive Poetry Analysis/Literary Device Learning Experience
- Chapter Review Learning Experience

I've also developed a "Literary Device Tool Kit" that has a list of some of my favorite literary/poetic devices. I provide definitions for each literary device and examples of how they work from my own lyrics and poems. This gives learners an opportunity to understand these concepts in a context that they'll recognize and appreciate. They'll use this tool kit in the Deep Dive Poetry Analysis Learning Experience to identify literary devices in the various poems in each chapter.

This work is very important to me and I hope it will be important to your learning space as well. A person doesn't have to be a Hip Hop expert to utilize this curriculum effectively. You do have to undergo some type of training on how to utilize the curriculum and to understand some of the rationale behind the approaches to the various Learning Experiences. I also want to develop a way for those who are utilizing the curriculum in their learning spaces to contribute to the evolution of the curriculum. Your experience with applying the curriculum and the responses of the learners to the curriculum will be extremely valuable in ensuring that we continue to work toward implementing curriculum that is culturally relevant and significant.

Recommended use of Curriculum

Since there are Learning Experiences that will be used in every chapter this is my recommendation for how to maximize the effectiveness of the curriculum.

Begin each chapter with the learners watching the video of the poem. Let them first watch the poem video. Allow them to watch the video again while reading the text of the poem. Encourage them to underline/highlight words or phrases that stick out to them, or they'd like to understand more.

1. Playlist to Black Boy Poems video: https://www.youtube.com/watch?v=nOHtIYU3a2s&list=PLCnHtWcSg3Hg3LP7m_IYWA4rnasNHqeLf

2. After watching and reading the video have the learners complete the **Initial Poem Response LE** to capture their ideas and reflections to the poem.

3. If you have a class session with a group of learners, feel free to have them participate in a group discussion based on their responses to the poem.

4. **Vocabulary LE** - this will give the learners a chance to engage with more of the language and references in the poem and chapter text.

5. After completing the Vocabulary LE have the learners read and watch the poem again and then do the **Second Poem Reflection LE**. (class discussion after the LE based upon their responses to the LE)

6. Read the section Reflections of a Black Boy and the essay for the chapter.

7. During the reading of the chapter, or after the chapter have the learners work on the **Unique LE(s)**. Some chapters have more than one unique LE. For those I'll also provide some advice for how to introduce them to the learning space. (class discussion after the LE) Depending on how many learners you have, you might choose to have the learners complete the LE as a group project.

8. After finishing the Unique LEs, you'll have the learners work on the **Deep Dive Poetry Analysis/Literary Device LE** (class discussion after the LE)

9. **Chapter Review LE** learners can use this LE as a summative experience for the poem and chapter. An extension LE from this chapter summary would be an essay response to the content of the poem and chapter. Other extension ideas are included in the Black Boy Poems Curriculum videos.

Common Core and Content Standards

Common Core Standards for Curriculum:

Key Ideas and Details:

CCSS.ELA-LITERACY.RI.9-10.1
Cite strong and thorough textual evidence to support analysis of what the text says explicitly as well as inferences drawn from the text.

CCSS.ELA-LITERACY.RI.9-10.2
Determine a central idea of a text and analyze its development over the course of the text, including how it emerges and is shaped and refined by specific details; provide an objective summary of the text.

CCSS.ELA-LITERACY.RI.11-12.1
Cite strong and thorough textual evidence to support analysis of what the text says explicitly as well as inferences drawn from the text, including determining where the text leaves matters uncertain.

CCSS.ELA-LITERACY.RI.11-12.2
Determine two or more central ideas of a text and analyze their development over the course of the text, including how they interact and build on one another to provide a complex analysis; provide an objective summary of the text.

Craft and Structure:

CCSS.ELA-LITERACY.RL.11-12.4
Determine the meaning of words and phrases as they are used in the text, including figurative and connotative meanings; analyze the impact of specific word choices on meaning and tone, including words with multiple meanings or language that is particularly fresh, engaging, or beautiful. (Include Shakespeare as well as other authors.)

CCSS.ELA-LITERACY.RL.11-12.5
Analyze how an author's choices concerning how to structure specific parts of a text (e.g., the choice of where to begin or end a story, the choice to provide a comedic or tragic resolution) contribute to its overall structure and meaning as well as its aesthetic impact.

9

<u>CCSS.ELA-LITERACY.RL.11-12.6</u>
Analyze a case in which grasping a point of view requires distinguishing what is directly stated in a text from what is really meant (e.g., satire, sarcasm, irony, or understatement).

Integration of Knowledge and Ideas:

<u>CCSS.ELA-LITERACY.RL.11-12.7</u>
Analyze multiple interpretations of a story, drama, or poem (e.g., recorded or live production of a play or recorded novel or poetry), evaluating how each version interprets the source text. (Include at least one play by Shakespeare and one play by an American dramatist.)

Range of Reading and Level of Text Complexity:

<u>CCSS.ELA-LITERACY.RL.11-12.10</u>
By the end of grade 11, read and comprehend literature, including stories, dramas, and poems, in the grades 11-CCR text complexity band proficiently, with scaffolding as needed at the high end of the range.

By the end of grade 12, read and comprehend literature, including stories, dramas, and poems, at the high end of the grades 11-CCR text complexity band independently and proficiently.

<u>CCSS.ELA-LITERACY.RI.9-10.3</u>
Analyze how the author unfolds an analysis or series of ideas or events, including the order in which the points are made, how they are introduced and developed, and the connections that are drawn between them.

<u>CCSS.ELA-LITERACY.RI.11-12.3</u>
Analyze a complex set of ideas or sequence of events and explain how specific individuals, ideas, or events interact and develop over the course of the text.

Craft and Structure:

<u>CCSS.ELA-LITERACY.RI.9-10.4</u>
Determine the meaning of words and phrases as they are used in a text, including figurative, connotative, and technical meanings; analyze the cumulative impact of specific word choices on meaning and tone (e.g., how the language of a court opinion differs from that of a newspaper).

CCSS.ELA-LITERACY.RI.11-12.4

Determine the meaning of words and phrases as they are used in a text, including figurative, connotative, and technical meanings; analyze how an author uses and refines the meaning of a key term or terms over the course of a text (e.g., how Madison defines faction in Federalist No. 10).

CCSS.ELA-LITERACY.RI.9-10.5

Analyze in detail how an author's ideas or claims are developed and refined by particular sentences, paragraphs, or larger portions of a text (e.g., a section or chapter).

CCSS.ELA-LITERACY.RI.11-12.5

Analyze and evaluate the effectiveness of the structure an author uses in his or her exposition or argument, including whether the structure makes points clear, convincing, and engaging.

CCSS.ELA-LITERACY.RI.9-10.6

Determine an author's point of view or purpose in a text and analyze how an author uses rhetoric to advance that point of view or purpose.

Integration of Knowledge and Ideas:

CCSS.ELA-LITERACY.RI.9-10.7

Analyze various accounts of a subject told in different mediums (e.g., a person's life story in both print and multimedia), determining which details are emphasized in each account.

CCSS.ELA-LITERACY.RI.9-10.8

Delineate and evaluate the argument and specific claims in a text, assessing whether the reasoning is valid and the evidence is relevant and sufficient; identify false statements and fallacious reasoning.

Range of Reading and Level of Text Complexity:

CCSS.ELA-LITERACY.RI.9-10.10

By the end of grade 9, read and comprehend literary nonfiction in the grades 9-10 text complexity band proficiently, with scaffolding as needed at the high end of the range. By the end of grade 10, read and comprehend literary nonfiction at the high end of the grades 9-10 text complexity band independently and proficiently.

Comprehension and Collaboration:

CCSS.ELA-LITERACY.SL.11-12.1
Initiate and participate effectively in a range of collaborative discussions (one-on-one, in groups, and teacher-led) with diverse partners on grades 11-12 topics, texts, and issues, building on others' ideas and expressing their own clearly and persuasively.

CCSS.ELA-LITERACY.SL.11-12.1.C
Propel conversations by posing and responding to questions that probe reasoning and evidence; ensure a hearing for a full range of positions on a topic or issue; clarify, verify, or challenge ideas and conclusions; and promote divergent and creative perspectives.

CCSS.ELA-LITERACY.SL.11-12.1.D
Respond thoughtfully to diverse perspectives; synthesize comments, claims, and evidence made on all sides of an issue; resolve contradictions when possible; and determine what additional information or research is required to deepen the investigation or complete the task.

CCSS.ELA-LITERACY.SL.11-12.2
Integrate multiple sources of information presented in diverse formats and media (e.g., visually, quantitatively, orally) in order to make informed decisions and solve problems, evaluating the credibility and accuracy of each source and noting any discrepancies among the data. (Review Mixed media LE)

CCSS.ELA-LITERACY.SL.11-12.3
Evaluate a speaker's point of view, reasoning, and use of evidence and rhetoric, assessing the stance, premises, links among ideas, word choice, points of emphasis, and tone used. (deep dive)

Text Types and Purposes:

CCSS.ELA-LITERACY.W.11-12.2

Write informative/explanatory texts to examine and convey complex ideas, concepts, and information clearly and accurately through the effective selection, organization, and analysis of content.

CCSS.ELA-LITERACY.W.11-12.2.B
Develop the topic thoroughly by selecting the most significant and relevant facts, extended definitions, concrete details, quotations, or other information and examples appropriate to the audience's knowledge of the topic.

CCSS.ELA-LITERACY.W.11-12.2.D
Use precise language, domain-specific vocabulary, and techniques such as metaphor, simile, and analogy to manage the complexity of the topic.

Research to Build and Present Knowledge:

CCSS.ELA-LITERACY.W.11-12.8
Gather relevant information from multiple authoritative print and digital sources, using advanced searches effectively; assess the strengths and limitations of each source in terms of the task, purpose, and audience; integrate information into the text selectively to maintain the flow of ideas, avoiding plagiarism and over reliance on any one source and following a standard format for citation.

Range of Writing:

CCSS.ELA-LITERACY.W.11-12.10
Write routinely over extended time frames (time for research, reflection, and revision) and shorter time frames (a single sitting or a day or two) for a range of tasks, purposes, and audiences.

Knowledge of Language:

CCSS.ELA-LITERACY.L.11-12.3
Apply knowledge of language to understand how language functions in different contexts, to make effective choices for meaning or style, and to comprehend more fully when reading or listening.

CCSS.ELA-LITERACY.L.11-12.3.A

Vary syntax for effect, consulting references (e.g., Tufte's Artful Sentences) for guidance as needed; apply an understanding of syntax to the study of complex texts when reading.

Vocabulary Acquisition and Use:

CCSS.ELA-LITERACY.L.11-12.4
Determine or clarify the meaning of unknown and multiple-meaning words and phrases based on grades 11-12 reading and content, choosing flexibly from a range of strategies.

CCSS.ELA-LITERACY.L.11-12.4.A
Use context (e.g., the overall meaning of a sentence, paragraph, or text; a word's position or function in a sentence) as a clue to the meaning of a word or phrase.

CCSS.ELA-LITERACY.L.11-12.5
Demonstrate understanding of figurative language, word relationships, and nuances in word meanings.

CCSS.ELA-LITERACY.L.11-12.5.A
Interpret figures of speech (e.g., hyperbole, paradox) in context and analyze their role in the text.

CCSS.ELA-LITERACY.L.11-12.5.B
Analyze nuances in the meaning of words with similar denotations.

History

Range of Reading and Level of Text Complexity:

CCSS.ELA-LITERACY.RH.11-12.10
By the end of grade 12, read and comprehend history/social studies texts in the grades 11-CCR text complexity band independently and proficiently.

Key Ideas and Details:

CCSS.ELA-LITERACY.RH.11-12.1

Cite specific textual evidence to support analysis of primary and secondary sources, connecting insights gained from specific details to an understanding of the text as a whole.

CCSS.ELA-LITERACY.RH.11-12.2
Determine the central ideas or information of a primary or secondary source; provide an accurate summary that makes clear the relationships among the key details and ideas.

CCSS.ELA-LITERACY.RH.11-12.3
Evaluate various explanations for actions or events and determine which explanation best accords with textual evidence, acknowledging where the text leaves matters uncertain.

Integration of Knowledge and Ideas:

CCSS.ELA-LITERACY.RH.11-12.7
Integrate and evaluate multiple sources of information presented in diverse formats and media (e.g., visually, quantitatively, as well as in words) in order to address a question or solve a problem.

CCSS.ELA-LITERACY.RH.11-12.8
Evaluate an author's premises, claims, and evidence by corroborating or challenging them with other information.

CCSS.ELA-LITERACY.RH.11-12.9
Integrate information from diverse sources, both primary and secondary, into a coherent understanding of an idea or event, noting discrepancies among sources.

Range of Reading and Level of Text Complexity:

CCSS.ELA-LITERACY.RH.11-12.10
By the end of grade 12, read and comprehend history/social studies texts in the grades 11-CCR text complexity band independently and proficiently.

Social Science Content Standards

Historical and Social Sciences Analysis Skills

The intellectual skills noted below are to be learned through, and applied to, the content standards for grades nine through twelve. They are to be assessed only in conjunction with the content standards in grades nine through twelve.

In addition to the standards for grades nine through twelve, students demonstrate the following intellectual, reasoning, reflection, and research skills.

Chronological and Spatial Thinking

1. Students compare the present with the past, evaluating the consequences of past events and decisions and determining the lessons that were learned.

2. Students analyze how change happens at different rates at different times; understand that some aspects can change while others remain the same; and understand that change is complicated and affects not only technology and politics but also values and beliefs.

3. Students use a variety of maps and documents to interpret human movement, including major patterns of domestic and international migration, changing environmental preferences and settlement patterns, the frictions that develop between population groups, and the diffusion of ideas, technological innovations, and goods.

4. Students relate current events to the physical and human characteristics of places and regions.

Historical Research, Evidence, and Point of View

1. Students distinguish valid arguments from fallacious arguments in historical interpretations.

2. Students identify bias and prejudice in historical interpretations.

3. Students evaluate major debates among historians concerning alternative interpretations of the past, including an analysis of authors' use of evidence and the distinctions be tween sound generalizations and misleading oversimplifications.

4. Students construct and test hypotheses; collect, evaluate, and employ information from multiple primary and secondary sources; and apply it in oral and written presentations.

Historical Interpretation

1. Students show the connections, causal and otherwise, between particular historical events and larger social, economic, and political trends and developments.

2. Students recognize the complexity of historical causes and effects, including the limitations on determining cause and effect.

3. Students interpret past events and issues within the context in which an event unfolded rather than solely in terms of present-day norms and values.

4. Students understand the meaning, implication, and impact of historical events and recognize that events could have taken other directions.

5. Students analyze human modifications of landscapes and examine the resulting environ mental policy issues.

6. Students conduct cost-benefit analyses and apply basic economic indicators to analyze the aggregate economic behavior of the U.S. economy.

10.3 Students analyze the effects of the Industrial Revolution in England, France, Germany, Japan, and the United States.

6. Analyze the emergence of capitalism as a dominant economic pattern and the responses to it, including Utopianism, Social Democracy, Socialism, and Communism.

10.4 Students analyze patterns of global change in the era of New Imperialism in at least two of the following regions or countries: Africa, Southeast Asia, China, India, Latin America, and the Philippines.

1. Describe the rise of industrial economies and their link to imperialism and colonial ism (e.g., the role played by national security and strategic advantage; moral issues raised by the search for national hegemony, Social Darwinism, and the missionary impulse; material issues such as land, resources, and technology).

2. Discuss the locations of the colonial rule of such nations as England, France, Germany, Italy, Japan, the Netherlands, Russia, Spain, Portugal, and the United States.

3. Explain imperialism from the perspective of the colonizers and the colonized and the varied immediate and long-term responses by the people under colonial rule.

11.2 Students analyze the relationship among the rise of industrialization, large-scale rural-to-urban migration, and massive immigration from Southern and Eastern Europe.

6. Trace the economic development of the United States and its emergence as a major industrial power, including its gains from trade and the advantages of its physical geography.

11.10 Students analyze the development of federal civil rights and voting rights.

2. Examine and analyze the key events, policies, and court cases in the evolution of civil rights, including Dred Scott v. Sandford, Plessy v. Ferguson, Brown v. Board of Education, Regents of the University of California v. Bakke, and California Proposition 209.

4. Examine the roles of civil rights advocates (e.g., A. Philip Randolph, Martin Luther King, Jr., Malcom X, Thurgood Marshall, James Farmer, Rosa Parks), including the significance of Martin Luther King, Jr.'s "Letter from Birmingham Jail" and "I Have a Dream" speech.

7. Analyze the women's rights movement from the era of Elizabeth Stanton and Susan Anthony and the passage of the Nineteenth Amendment to the movement launched in the 1960s, including differing perspectives on the roles of women.

11.11 Students analyze the major social problems and domestic policy issues in contemporary American society.

1. Discuss the reasons for the nation's changing immigration policy, with emphasis on how the Immigration Act of 1965 and successor acts have transformed American society.

3. Describe the changing roles of women in society as reflected in the entry of more women into the labor force and the changing family structure.

6. Analyze the persistence of poverty and how different analyses of this issue influence welfare reform, health insurance reform, and other social policies.

7. Explain how the federal, state, and local governments have responded to demographic and social changes such as population shifts to the suburbs, racial concentra tions in the cities, Frostbelt-to-Sunbelt migration, international migration, decline of family farms, increases in out-of-wedlock births, and drug abuse.

12.5 Students summarize landmark U.S. Supreme Court interpretations of the Constitution and its amendments.

1. Understand the changing interpretations of the Bill of Rights over time, including interpretations of the basic freedoms (religion, speech, press, petition, and assembly) articulated in the First Amendment and the due process and equal-protection-of-the- law clauses of the Fourteenth Amendment.

4. Explain the controversies that have resulted over changing interpretations of civil rights, including those in Plessy v. Ferguson, Brown v. Board of Education, Miranda v. Arizona, Regents of the University of California v. Bakke, Adarand Constructors, Inc. v. Pena, and United States v. Virginia (VMI).

Principles of Economics

12.1 Students understand common economic terms and concepts and economic reasoning.

1. Examine the causal relationship between scarcity and the need for choices.

4. Evaluate the role of private property as an incentive in conserving and improving scarce resources, including renewable and nonrenewable natural resources.

5. Analyze the role of a market economy in establishing and preserving political and personal liberty (e.g., through the works of Adam Smith).

12.2 Students analyze the elements of America's market economy in a global setting.

8. Explain the role of profit as the incentive to entrepreneurs in a market economy.

9. Describe the functions of the financial markets.

12.3 Students analyze the influence of the federal government on the American economy.

1. Understand how the role of government in a market economy often includes providing for national defense, addressing environmental concerns, defining and enforcing property rights, attempting to make markets more competitive, and protecting consumers' rights.

12.4 Students analyze the elements of the U.S. labor market in a global setting.

2. Describe the current economy and labor market, including the types of goods and services produced, the types of skills workers need, the effects of rapid technological change, and the impact of international competition.

12.6 Students analyze issues of international trade and explain how the U.S. economy affects, and is affected by, economic forces beyond the United States's borders.

3. Understand the changing role of international political borders and territorial sovereignty in a global economy.

Common Learning Experiences

Black Boy Poems Initial Poetry Reflection Learning Experience

Poem title:

_____

1. Write down your initial/immediate thoughts and feelings about the poem.

2. In what ways do your lived experiences or the lived experiences of those around you allow you to connect with the content in the poem? Explain.

3. Write down any words or references in the poem that you'd like to get a better understanding of.

Poem title:

_____

1. Choose a quote from the section "Reflections of a Black Boy" for the poem you're analyzing. Copy the quote here (if it's long, you can use "..." to show the quote continues.)

2. Which line or lines from the poem are connected to this quote you chose? Explain the connection.

3. What ideas do you think Tyson Amir is expressing here in this section? What are your personal responses to his ideas? What personal experiences in your life does this reflection remind you of?

Black Boy Poems Second Poetry Reflection Learning Experience

Poem title:

_____

1. Choose a line or lines from the poem that you connected with. Copy the lines here (if they are long, you can use "..." to show the line(s) continues.)

2. In what ways do you connect with the lines that you selected based on your personal experience/perspective? What about the lines makes them stand out to you?

3. What message do you think the author was attempting to convey in the poem, and more specifically in the lines you selected? What do you think is the overall message of the poem? Do you feel Tyson was successful in delivering that message?

Black Boy Poems Poetry Analysis Learning Experience

Poetry Analysis (Watch the video and read the text of the poem)

1. Based on the setting created by the author in the poem, what is the timeframe the poem is set in? What do you know about the context of that era that might have influenced the writing of this poem?

2. What significance do you feel the title has in this piece? Do you feel it was an appropriate title for the poem? Explain. Why do you think Tyson chose this to be the title of the poem? What other title do you feel would be appropriate for this poem? Explain.

3. How would you describe the mood/tone of the poem? What lines/ phrases in the poem help to illustrate the mood/tone?

4. What imagery/sensory language does the poem contain? Give a few examples. What meanings does the imagery/sensory language convey in the poem, and to you?

5. What are the most powerful themes communicated in the poem? Provide examples from the poem. Explain why you feel these themes are powerful.

6. How would you describe the meaning/significance of this poem in your own words to someone else? In what ways does it connect with other material you've studied inside and outside of school? Do you feel the poem is still relevant today? Explain why.

Black Boy Poems Literary Devices Kit Learning Experience

Literary Device Tool Kit:

Alliteration - Assonance - Anthropomorphism - Circumlocution - Double & Triple Entendre - Homophone - Idiom - Imagery - Jargon/Vernacular - Juxtaposition - Metaphor - Multi Syllable Rhyme - Personification - Repetition - Schematic/Thematic Writing - Simile - Advanced Alliteration*

Identify at least 3 literary devices in this poem. (Write the names of the devices below)

1. _____

2. _____

3. _____

Quote the lines that contain the literary devices.

_____

_____

_____

_____

_____

_____

_____

_____

_____

Experiment with literary devices

- Pick one of the literary devices from above and write a short response in lyric, poem or prose form. Incorporate that literary device in your response.

Black Boy Poems Chapter Review Learning Experience

Chapter Review

1. Write down the thoughts, reactions and connections that you had with the content in the chapter?

2. What are the major points that Tyson Amir is attempting to articulate in this chapter? (Major themes, arguments, historical/statistical information and any other valuable points)

3. What new information/insights do you feel you received from the poem, reflection and content in this chapter? Explain.

4. What quotes/selections from the chapter stood out to you? Copy the lines down and express why they stood out to you.

5. In what ways do you see connections between your lived experience and the themes and content in the chapter? In what ways do you see connections between the content of the chapter and what is taking place in our society today? Explain

6. Give a brief summary of the chapter. Use at least two references from the chapter essay to support your summary of the text.

"41 Shots"

41 Shots

A very strong element that is present in much of my work is the idea of social/ political commentary. Your learners might or might not be familiar with that concept. I believe it's a very important concept to introduce when beginning the Black Boy Poems Curriculum.

"41 Shots" is a powerful example of what social/political commentary can look like. I was still a teenager when I wrote the poem. The tragic murder of Amadou Diallo compelled me to voice my anger, frustrations, sorrow and fears. It took the form of a poem that made a strong commentary and critique of society in that moment.

Themes:

There are several themes that are important to highlight before the learners start working on the Learning Experiences.

- State Violence (when a state/government institution commits acts of violence)

- Accountability (What is accountability, and what does it look like when a harm occurs?)

- Migration (Diallo's family migrated to the United States in the early 1990s. What are the challenges, causes and consequences of migration? What's the experience of migrating to a new place where you instantly become a feared minority?)

- Black Lives Matter (Diallo's murder occurred before the birth of the BLM movement, however his murder was protested, discussed and debated far and wide.)

- Police Violence

- Injustice on behalf of the state.

Prerequisites and Scaffolding:

- Students should be given some background information on Amadou Diallo.

- I believe it's extremely important to highlight the migrant experience that his family went through leaving West Africa for New York. This is an opportunity to allow learners who also come from families with migrant stories to connect on a deeper level with the content.

- The experience of migrating to a place where being African or Black has an entirely different meaning.

Implementation of Curriculum:

1. Initial Poem Reflection Learning Experience

2. Vocabulary Learning Experience

3. Second Poem Reflection Learning Experience

4. Unique Learning Experience: 41 Shots

This LE asks the learners to research names mentioned in the poem. I reference multiple names in the poem paralleling their experiences with Amadou Diallo. Students will research these other names and learn more about the general context that produced the poem.

Learners will be asked to use different sources for their research. A general article, news article and video source. As an instructor you can help reinforce what sources are viewed as more "respected" or "trustworthy". Allow the learners to use those different sources to respond to the research questions in the LE.

I suggest allowing the learners flexibility in how they compose and deliver their responses. Here are a few examples: podcast, blog, video presentation, written response or any other acceptable form for your learning space.

5. Deep Dive Poetry Analysis/Literary Device Learning Experience

6. Chapter Review Learning Experience

Expansion LEs

Here are a few opportunities for further discussion and exploration.

- How to hold the government/state/authority figures accountable?

- Examples of law enforcement in other parts of the world

- Other ways communities have developed methods of protecting their citizens.

- Community Policing

Chronological and Spatial Thinking

Students relate current events to the physical and human characteristics of places and regions.
Historical Research, Evidence, and Point of View

Students identify bias and prejudice in historical interpretations.

Students construct and test hypotheses; collect, evaluate, and employ information from multiple primary and secondary sources; and apply it in oral and written presentations.

Historical Interpretation

Students show the connections, causal and otherwise, between particular historical events and larger social, economic, and political trends and developments.

Students recognize the complexity of historical causes and effects, including the limitations on determining cause and effect.

Students interpret past events and issues within the context in which an event unfolded rather than solely in terms of present-day norms and values.

Students understand the meaning, implication, and impact of historical events and recognize that events could have taken other directions.

Students analyze the major social problems and domestic policy issues in contemporary American society.

Standards and Learning objectives

Students analyze the development of federal civil rights and voting rights.

1. Explain how demands of African Americans helped produce a stimulus for civil rights, including President Roosevelt's ban on racial discrimination in defense industries in 1941, and how African Americans' service in World War II produced a stimulus for President Truman's decision to end segregation in the armed forces in 1948.

2. Examine and analyze the key events, policies, and court cases in the evolution of civil rights, including Dred Scott v. Sandford, Plessy v. Ferguson, Brown v. Board of Education, Regents of the University of California v. Bakke, and California Proposition 209.

4. Examine the roles of civil rights advocates (e.g., A. Philip Randolph, Martin Luther King, Jr., Malcom X, Thurgood Marshall, James Farmer, Rosa Parks), including the significance of Martin Luther King, Jr.'s "Letter from Birmingham Jail" and "I Have a Dream" speech.

Discuss the diffusion of the civil rights movement of African Americans from the churches of the rural South and the urban North, including the resistance to racial desegregation in Little Rock and Birmingham, and how the advances influenced the agendas, strategies, and effectiveness of the quests of American Indians, Asian Americans, and Hispanic Americans for civil rights and equal opportunities.

1. Discuss the reasons for the nation's changing immigration policy, with emphasis on how the Immigration Act of 1965 and successor acts have transformed American society.

2. Trace the origins and development of slavery; its effects on black Americans and on the region's political, social, religious, economic, and cultural development; and identify the strategies that were tried to both overturn and preserve it (e.g., through the writings and historical documents on Nat Turner, Denmark Vesey).

41 Shots (1999)

I speak to beats composed of African cries,
spilled indigenous blood,
horrified shrieks,
prison doors locking,
legalized lynchings,
police ammunition flying through the skies
to contact black skin.
Let's examine that last line once again.
Police ammunition flying through the skies
to contact black skin.
My Name is Amadou Diallo.
41 shots.
I was hit
19 times.
These are simply the facts.
Now we are forced to ask the question,
what was my crime?
Some say guilty of being black,
I agree.
I see 4 plain clothes police officers
I mean pigs
approach me
and ask me for my I.D.
I oblige.
They reply
with 41 shots.
I was hit
19 times.
The first shot severed my spine in 4 different places,
paralysis starts to set in.
I can no longer stand,
an unarmed black man
lying on the floor,
never to them was I a threat,
but they still
feel the need to fire 40 more shots.
Stop!
Whatever happened to
innocent until proven guilty?
Yet I am fatally wounded and filthy
covered in the blood of my ancestors.
I came in search
of a better life
the American Dream,
but Immigration never told me about the 500 year history of this racist nation.
I never heard about brothers and sisters like

Rodney King,
Tyisha Miller,
Abner Louima,
Fred Hampton,
George Jackson,
Bobby Hutton,
Emmett Till.
Still I say
I've committed no crime,
but it's illegal to be black in this country.
Where they call me
monkey,
coon,
and baboon,
and scientist create theories to prove the inferiority of my skin tone.
And police officers named
pork-chop,
piglet,
pork rind,
and swine
legally lynch me
to assassinate my 46 chromosomes.
That's state sponsored genocide.
I can't even safely walk into my home.

41 shots
19 hits
a 46% hit ratio.
Now do you see how these stereo-typical
beliefs affect me here
with the fears they associate with black people
on movies, television, and radio.
Black people are dumb,
black people are addicted to drugs,
black people are thugs with guns.
This is how come
4 armed pigs can be afraid
and fire 41 standard state issued nigger killers
with the intention to kill just one.
Innocent, unarmed brother,
I say it's because
I'm a Black Man!

Vocabulary Study Chart: "41 Shots"

Word	Definition(s) and Synonym(s)	Copy the line or sentence from the text.	Your own example sentence
Composed			
Indigenous			
Lynching			
Oblige			

Word	Definition(s) and Synonym(s)	Copy the line or sentence from the text.	Your own example sentence
Sever			
Paralysis			
Chromosomes			
Genocide			

Word	Definition(s) and Synonym(s)	Copy the line or sentence from the text.	Your own example sentence
Abolition			
Unprecedented			
Disenfranchised			
Discern			

Word	Definition(s) and Synonym(s)	Copy the line or sentence from the text.	Your own example sentence
Exonerate			
Akin			

Black Boy Poems Research Learning Experience

In the poem **41 Shots** Tyson Amir mentions a number of names comparing their experiences with Amadou Diallo. The goal of this LE is to become more familiar with the context of each name mentioned, and for learners to use their critical analysis to make connections between their cases.

Learners will research each name using at least three different sources.

1. General article (i.e wikipedia or blogs) (These are great for general information but are not considered verified news sources)

2. News article (From a verified news source. Keep in mind that even "news" sources can be biased in their reporting of events.)

3. Video (News broadcast or documentary on subject)

List your sources and answer the following questions.

1. When and where did the person live, die and or have their negative interaction with the state?

2. Where did their encounter with members of the community/ law enforcement take place? What was the "alleged" reason for the encounter? What happened in the encounter?

3. What was the political significance of the person and the encounter? How did society, law enforcement and the government respond? Was anybody held accountable for what transpired?

Critical analysis

4. What connections do you see between this person and Amadou Diallo? What connections do you see with any of the other names on this list?

5. Have you or anyone you know ever encountered anything similar to one of these figures you researched? If so, how did the community respond to the incident? Was anyone held accountable for what happened?

Names to research:

Amadou Diallo

Rodney King

Tyisha Miller

Abner Louima

Fred Hampton

George Jackson

Bobby Hutton

Emmett Till

"Family Tree"

Family Tree

This is a very powerful poem. Family Tree is the first of a few story poems in Black Boy Poems. The narrative is all true. It might be a good idea to give the learners advanced notice about the potential for the piece to create deep emotional reactions/responses to the content.

Themes:

These are some of the themes that I believe are important to highlight before and during the exploration of the chapter.

- Addiction (causes and consequences)

- Family (keeping in mind that your learners might have very different experiences with family. As well as, very different definitions of family.)

- Intergenerational impact and trauma (Epigenetics)

- Inheritance (what we receive from those before us)

- Chemical warfare

- A more fertile soil (what do we choose to carry on from what was given to us to help create a more fertile soil for the next generation.)

Prerequisites and Scaffolding:

- The Power of narrative. I inherited a culture that emphasized oral tradition as a primary way of communicating and learning. A gripping narrative can be a powerful tool for learning and documentation. This poem provides a foundation for appreciation of oral traditions, story and narrative. I provide a first person account of an experience in my family. There is a power in being able to tell stories. Being able to shed light on experiences that we sometimes are made to feel should be kept quiet.

- As mentioned in the previous section, the concept of family could be a little sensitive for some of our learners. However, the piece focuses on a family tree and some of the struggles a family faced for generations. In this regard the concept of family tree is extremely important to understand. The good, bad and other aspects of it.

- Great Migration(s) - the trips made by blacks to flee the oppressive conditions of the south. This also connects with the idea of forced migrations.

- Racism experienced by blacks in the armed services

Implementation of Curriculum:

1. Initial Poem Reflection Learning Experience

2. Vocabulary Learning Experience

3. Second Poem Reflection Learning Experience

4. Unique Learning Experiences: Family Tree

This section has two unique LEs.

More Fertile Soil
This LE has reflective and critical thinking components. The LE allows the learners to examine what has been passed on to them by "family" and "community/society". After reflecting on both areas, they then have to decide what they will choose to carry forward with them to create a more fertile soil. This LE is a great way to build strong relationships and a culture or compassion, tolerance and understanding in the learning space.

Chemical Warfare
This is a research based LE that allows the learners to explore historical examples of "chemical warfare" and its impact. The research methodology is similar to the one used in 41 Shots. Allow the students to select which topics they'd like to research and guide them in their research as they move through the different topics responding to the research and critical thinking questions.

I strongly recommend having the learners look at then Senator John Kerry's report in 1989, as well as the articles published in the San Jose Mercury News in 1996 by Gary Webb as ways of finding resources that were published during or close to the actual incidents that took place if they're researching the topic on California.

5. Deep Dive Poetry Analysis/Literary Device Learning Experience

6. Chapter Review Learning Experience

Expansion LEs:

Family Tree LE for learners. (let them create a story about their family tree)

Who are the winners and losers in the US Drug War

Family Tree

Chronological and Spatial Thinking

Students compare the present with the past, evaluating the consequences of past events and decisions and determining the lessons that were learned.

Students analyze how change happens at different rates at different times; understand that some aspects can change while others remain the same; and understand that change is complicated and affects not only technology and politics but also values and beliefs.

Students relate current events to the physical and human characteristics of places and regions.

Historical Research, Evidence, and Point of View

Students distinguish valid arguments from fallacious arguments in historical interpretations.

Students construct and test hypotheses; collect, evaluate, and employ information from multiple primary and secondary sources; and apply it in oral and written presentations.

Historical Interpretation

Students show the connections, causal and otherwise, between particular historical events and larger social, economic, and political trends and developments.

Students recognize the complexity of historical causes and effects, including the limitations on determining cause and effect.

Students interpret past events and issues within the context in which an event unfolded rather than solely in terms of present-day norms and values.

Students understand the meaning, implication, and impact of historical events and recognize that events could have taken other directions.

Standards and Learning objectives

Identify the roles and sacrifices of individual American soldiers, as well as the unique contributions of the special fighting forces (e.g., the Tuskegee Airmen, the 442nd Regimental Combat team, the Navajo Code Talkers).

4. Compare the lives of and opportunities for free blacks in the North with those of free blacks in the South.

6. Describe the lives of free blacks and the laws that limited their freedom and economic opportunities.

Family Tree (2000)

This is the story of my Grandfather.
When my Mom was still a toddler,
her mother married a man named John Oliver,
And like many black men
he worked in the armed service,
it's hard to determine
what made him nourish
his habit
of alcohol which made him an addict.
The travesty
of alcohol dependency
which led to a tendency
for a beast to surface
he would eventually
begin to
beat,
choke,
cuss,
hit,
whip,
inflict pain.
A young black man
intelligent and handsome,
but destined
to reclaim the anthem
of souls destroyed by those liquid phantoms.
He consumed demons and spirits
with stickers and labels.
Liquor,
in tinted glass containers.
Became a stranger to self
it changed his mentality,
became hellish
a drunken zealot
without any inhibition.
His mission
to satisfy his selfish desires
he struggled with his sobriety.
Even denying that he
had a problem.
When off the liquor,
sober,
he was one of the nicest men that you would ever meet.
He was kind,
generous,
considerate

but you see those times were
few and
far in between.
He developed a routine
on Fridays
to be gone for a few days
return home early Sundays.
The booze he paid for
stayed on his breath,
and the bruises he made
became sore
and stayed on her flesh.
As he led his family through the church doors
and played the role of the righteous father,
pious.
When he really had a dark side
of a pirate
a tyrant.
I call him a domestic terrorist,
all that violence and abuse
sanctioned
under the guidelines
of legal marriages.
My grandma sought counseling,
she went down to the local parish
and the church father told her like this,
to simply, "grin and bear it".
As if
God wanted her to be a punching bag for this man.
through
sickness and health
until death do you part,
but she stayed strong
knowing something was way wrong
and kept praying to God for help
because this man couldn't control himself.
Her mental health and life on the line
and at times
when intoxicated
you could see the devil in his eyes.
My aunt, uncles and mom would huddle and cry.
Hearing muffled blows on my grandma's flesh
not knowing if she'd be alive at the time of sunrise.
His inequities then spread to his seeds.
You see,
my aunt and two uncles began to emulate his deeds.
They started with the drinking and smoking,
but two of them didn't let it control them.
They conquered the monster,

but the addiction was so much stronger in my Uncle Johnny.
He named after his father,
he took after his father
and sought something to curb his addiction.
He started experimenting
injected heroin into his system through his forearm.
One shot was all that it took,
hook,
line
and sinker.
He destined from the womb
to be a casualty of this chemical warfare.
The family noticed he drastically changed.
His parents already gone their separate way.
You see
my grandma finally got the divorce.
John Oliver Sr.
he out in Mississippi
he tipsy of course.
Little Johnny was figity,
he wasn't into as much physical activity
as he used be.
And what could it be the family would ask,
Nothing!
is what he'd snap back
but it became all apparent when he forged his mom's signature to get cash
that he had smack tracks
on the other side of his elbow.
He got into a rehab
and started getting back to the Johnny we used to know
but then them chemicals
began to call him back
by way of this one fast sister he used to holler at.
You see,
she slipped him a bag of smack
that wasn't cut clean
set to wreck havoc in his recovering bloodstream.
Still he cooked it,
he drew it up slow into the syringe.
Tied his arm off tight,
pushed that needle through his skin.
My poor Uncle Johnny,
he chasing that dragon again,
and that evening this is what happened to him.
He shot up,
he dropped
to his knees.
His muscles seized up,
his heart gave up

he never got up
he a byproduct of his father's disease.
And by now
under his skin,
his blood starts to chill.
In sets the rigor mortis.
my uncle,
he a picture,
a ghetto still portrait
titled:
"Overdose in mom's kitchen".
My grandma
she comes home tired from work
not knowing his condition.
Not knowing that her worst nightmare has just
come to fruition.
It's dark inside the home
the light switch is on the other side of the room.
She feels an emptiness in her womb
as she passes a cold stump.
She calls out for Johnny
there's no answer
he's not responding,
she turns the light on
and sees her son's body hunched over
with his life gone.
And that night
my mom
felt the same pain so many miles away.
About a year later
I join the family.
And I'm the first after Johnny,
and somehow because of this madness
I know our bodies are
oddly connected.
John Oliver Sr. still just as reckless,
still drinking
still changing from a man into a demon.
Still scheming on women,
but one evening
it all began to catch up.
Payback for all them times
and all them lives
he done messed up.
And for real
it's hard to feel any remorse or sadness,
I still don't know all the details
but a woman who grew tired of his madness
took him off this planet for good.

Should I feel this way?
Truthfully, I don't even know.
All I know is that this is a true tale,
some of that ghetto non-fiction,
of what happened to my family
and all because of addiction.
Addiction, y'all
this is my family tree.

Vocabulary Study Chart: "Family Tree"

Word	Definition(s) and Synonym(s)	Copy the line or sentence from the text.	Your own example sentence
Nourish			
Travesty			
Anthem			
Spirits			

Word	Definition(s) and Synonym(s)	Copy the line or sentence from the text.	Your own example sentence
Zealot			
Inhibition			
Sobriety			
Sanctioned			

Word	Definition(s) and Synonym(s)	Copy the line or sentence from the text.	Your own example sentence
Iniquities			
Casualty			
Emulate			
Rigor mortis			

Word	Definition(s) and Synonym(s)	Copy the line or sentence from the text.	Your own example sentence
Rearing			
Inoculate			
Fruition			

Black Boy Poems Research Learning Experience

Creating a more fertile soil

In the quest for creating a more "fertile soil" it is essential that we know the strengths and weaknesses of who we are and what we inherited. A quote from the text *Black Boy Poems* that speaks to this point is from the military strategist Sun Tzu.

"It is said that if you know your enemies and know yourself, you will not be imperiled in a hundred battles; if you do not know your enemies but do know yourself, you will win one and lose one; if you do not know your enemies nor yourself, you will be imperiled in every single battle."

What you've inherited from your tree.

Answer these questions about your family

1. What "positive" cultural, social aspects have been passed down your family tree? Where did they come from? How have they benefited your family and you?

2. What "negative" cultural, social aspects have been passed down your family tree? Where did they come from? How have they impacted your family and you?

3. In light of these "positive" and "negative" aspects which do you want to carry and share with your community and the following generations? Explain why you selected these and how you plan to use them.

Answer these questions about the community you're from.

4. What positive cultural, social aspects are found in your community? Where did they come from? How have they benefited you and your community?

5. What "negative" cultural, social aspects have been found in your community? Where did they come from? How have they impacted you and your community?

6. In light of these "positive" and "negative" aspects which do you want to carry and share with your community and the following generations? Explain why you select these and how you plan to use them.

7. In what ways do you believe these things you've inherited and decided to carry on will contribute to a more "fertile soil"?

Black Boy Poems Research Learning Experience

In the poem "Family Tree," Tyson Amir says about his Uncle Johnny the he was, "destined from the womb to be a casualty of this chemical warfare." In this LE we'll explore the concept of chemical warfare. Upon completing this LE learners will have a better understanding of chemical warfare, how it has impacted peoples around the world and some of the major consequences and impacts of chemical warfare on specific communities.

Prior Knowledge:

What is your definition of chemical warfare?

What do you think is the author's definition of the concept of chemical warfare based on how he uses it in the poem? In what ways is your definition similar or different than the author's definition of it.

What historic or contemporary examples of chemical warfare are you familiar with?

Research three cases of chemical warfare and/or substance abuse impacting communities (one of them should be The Opium War, and two additional ones of your choice). Use at least three different sources, such as the following:

A. Information Website Source - (encyclopedia or other reference source you and your teacher agree upon)

B. Social Media Source - Twitter, Facebook, Snapchat, etc..

C. Verified News Source in Print (article) - CNN, CBS, Fox News, Univision, etc.. (From a verified news source. Keep in mind that even "news" sources can be biased in their reporting of events.)

D. Video Source - Documentary, film, news broadcast

Research Topics

1. The Opium War (different from the Opioid Crisis)

2. Alcohol and its impact on Indigenous/ Native communities

3. Reagan's Cocaine, California and the Contras.

4. The Sackler Family and the Opioid Crisis

For each of the cases that you research, answer the following questions:

Questions:

1. Who is/was involved in this case (for example, what countries, governments, politicians, celebrities, groups of people, etc…)? When and where did it take place? What chemicals were involved?

2. What population(s) are greatly affected by this chemical warfare case? What was the motivation behind introducing this substance to that population? How did the population respond to being exposed to this substance? Who was responsible for administering the substance?

3. What were the social, economic, criminal, and political consequences to the population consuming the substance? Were these consequences merited? Explain why.

4. Was anyone ever held accountable for this act of chemical warfare? Explain what happened and why you believe it happened that way.

5. Are the people who were principally affected by these instances of chemical warfare still dealing with consequences steaming from this event? Explain.

Possible resources

https://www.ncbi.nlm.nih.gov/pmc/articles/PMC1446168/pdf/10705850.pdf

https://www.recovery.org/topics/native-americans-alcoholism/

Opium War

https://www.youtube.com/watch?v=qHmuuc7m1AA

https://pubs.niaaa.nih.gov/publications/arh22-4/253.pdf

History of heroin

https://www.narconon.org/drug-information/heroin-history.html

https://www.cfr.org/backgrounder/us-opioid-epidemic

US Opiod Crisis

https://www.drugabuse.gov/drugs-abuse/opioids/opioid-overdose-crisis

Crack cocaine

https://www.salon.com/2004/10/25/contra/

But almost a decade later, in 1998, Kerry's trailblazing investigation was vindicated by the CIA's own inspector general, who found that scores of Contra operatives were implicated in the cocaine trade and that U.S. agencies had looked the other way rather than reveal information that could have embarrassed the Reagan-Bush administration.

Even after the CIA's admissions, the national press corps never fully corrected its earlier dismissive treatment. That would have meant the New York Times and other leading publications admitting they had bungled their coverage of one of the worst scandals of the Reagan-Bush era.

http://www.cnn.com/US/9811/03/cia.drugs/

https://www.huffingtonpost.com/2014/10/10/gary-webb-dark-alliance_n_5961748.html

In 1984, CIA received allegations that five individuals associated with the Democratic Revolutionary Alliance (ARDE)/Sandino Revolutionary Front (FRS) were engaged in a drug trafficking conspiracy with a known narcotics trafficker, Jorge Morales," the report found. "CIA broke off contact with ARDE in October 1984, but continued to have contact through 1986-87 with four of the individuals involved with Morales."

It also found that in October 1982, an immigration officer reported that, according to an informant in the Nicaraguan exile community in the Bay Area, "there are indications of links between [a specific U.S.-based religious organization] and two Nicaraguan counter-revolutionary groups. These links involve an exchange in [the United States] of narcotics for arms, which then are shipped to Nicaragua. A meeting on this matter is scheduled to be held in Costa Rica 'within one month.' Two names the informant has associated with this matter are Bergman Arguello, a UDN member and exile living in San Francisco, and Chicano Cardenal, resident of Nicaragua."

The inspector general is clear that in some cases "CIA knowledge of allegations or information indicating that organizations or individuals had been involved in drug trafficking did not deter their use by CIA." In other cases, "CIA did not act to verify drug trafficking allegations or information even when it had the opportunity to do so."
"Let me be frank about what we are finding," the CIA's inspector general, Frederick Hitz, said in congressional testimony in March 1998. "There are instances where CIA did not, in an expeditious or consistent fashion, cut off relationships with individuals supporting the Contra program who were alleged to have engaged in drug trafficking activity or take action to resolve the allegations."

Black Boy Poems Curriculum

"Under a Different Light"

Under a Different Light

This is another narrative based piece. It is the only piece in the collection that is a work of fiction. It's a combination of science fiction and historical fiction. Which provides an opportunity for learners to explore different genres of writing and expression. It's also an opportunity to reexamine the power of narrative for delivering a message.

I like this piece because it was inspired by Octavia Butler's science fiction writing. I usually write very straightforward social/political commentary but this piece came out different.

Themes:

- Science fiction motifs (this piece allows you to explore the concept of motif in writing, especially the alternate self motif which I use in this poem)

- Empathy is an important theme in the piece. The goal of the piece is to get the reader/listener to understand that they easily could've been someone else. Especially someone that they might look down on for whatever reason.

Prerequisites and Scaffolding:

- This is the only "fiction" piece I have in the entire collection of poems. The piece is definitely based in real world experiences but I use fiction to highlight the contradictions in our society. This piece demonstrates how fiction can be used to make commentary on society. (Uncle Tom's Cabin, 1984, Brave New World, Things Fall Apart, Kindred, Native Son)

- That F on my record stood out like a scarlet letter on my chest. F is slang for felony.

- Disenfranchisement of people who are formerly incarcerated. Making sure the learners are familiar with aspects of that experience. Especially black and brown people who are formerly incarcerated.

- Prison Industrial Complex (PIC)

- The understanding that slavery has never been illegal in the entire history of the United States. The 13th amendment abolished a specific type of slavery and still allowed for slavery to continue if a person is "convicted" of a crime in a court of law. Analyze the 13th amendment and it's connection to the current PIC.

Implementation of Curriculum:

1. Initial Poem Reflection Learning Experience

2. Vocabulary Learning Experience

3. Second Poem Reflection Learning Experience

4. Unique Learning Experiences: Under a Different Light

This section has two unique LEs.

Scarlet Letter LE
Compare and contrast the main character of *The Scarlet Letter* with the second character in the poem. In my opinion this is a great way to combine a text that many learners are forced to read in classes with an experience that many learners will understand in today's society. It will allow them to use their own experience to connect with a story written in a completely different social, cultural and political context. It will also allow them to seek parallels between different lived experiences.

Under a Different Light Research LE
The poem focuses heavily on the concept of empathy. This LE will give learners an opportunity to look at the different and sometimes more dangerous life possibilities for their fellow learners because of the "demographic" that they are defined as by society. My hope is that learners will be moved to want to work for a more just and equitable society after seeing the disparate experiences of their fellow learners. You might have to assist them with some of the research once they figure out the different groups they'll be compiling data on.

5. Deep Dive Poetry Analysis/Literary Device Learning Experience

6. Chapter Review Learning Experience

Expansion LEs

What are other scarlet letters in today's society?

Understanding the severity of the disenfranchisement that incarcerated and formerly incarcerated peoples experience. What are some of the things you can no longer do if you are formerly incarcerated?

Under a Different Light

Chronological and Spatial Thinking

Students compare the present with the past, evaluating the consequences of past events and decisions and determining the lessons that were learned.

Students analyze how change happens at different rates at different times; understand that some aspects can change while others remain the same; and understand that change is complicated and affects not only technology and politics but also values and beliefs.

Historical Research, Evidence, and Point of View

Students construct and test hypotheses; collect, evaluate, and employ information from multiple primary and secondary sources; and apply it in oral and written presentations.

Historical Interpretation

Students recognize the complexity of historical causes and effects, including the limitations on determining cause and effect.

Students interpret past events and issues within the context in which an event unfolded rather than solely in terms of present-day norms and values.

Students understand the meaning, implication, and impact of historical events and recognize that events could have taken other directions.

Standards and Learning objectives

6. Analyze the passage and effects of civil rights and voting rights legislation (e.g., 1964 Civil Rights Act, Voting Rights Act of 1965) and the Twenty-Fourth Amendment, with an emphasis on equality of access to education and to the political process.

6. Analyze the persistence of poverty and how different analyses of this issue influence welfare reform, health insurance reform, and other social policies.

7. Explain how the federal, state, and local governments have responded to demographic and social changes such as population shifts to the suburbs, racial concentrations in the cities, Frostbelt-to-Sunbelt migration, international migration, decline of family farms, increases in out-of-wedlock births, and drug abuse.

Under a Different Light (2001)

One day,
I was sitting at the dock of the bay.
This cat walked up listening to some Dr. Dre
and I thought about walking away,
but he caught me awkward way.
It's hard to explain
so I decided to engage
this man in some conversation.
His hair was braided into some cornrows,
he wore a jacket for the cold
with a cubic zirconia on his left earlobe.
And he strolled like a gangster
with the infamous
hop in his step.
Face contorted by anger,
my hypothesis
was a relationship
or his pockets weren't looking right.
He sat without acknowledging me
but it didn't bother me
because it was obvious to see
The he was preoccupied by the thoughts running through his mind.
We're all captives in this ball of confusion
for a period of time
trying to find solutions
invisible to the human eye.
I kept one eye on his body language
but stayed focused on the most beautiful skyline that the creator ever painted.
Contemplating
the beauties of this world,
but I still noticed when he
inhaled deep.
He startled me
once he started to speak
under his breath saying,
"man, something's gotta change, this madness gotta end, I can't do this no more."
He caught my attention
because I know desperation when I hear it from prior experience
so I joined his conversation
and gave him a salutation,
"Peace be unto you."
I had seemed to
catch him off guard
but he regained his composure quickly
and said specifically
"A yo, what does that mean?"

I replied, "truthfully,
the most important thing
because we all need peace to survive,
and even though I don't know you personally
I still wish for peace in your life,
and that's the first thing
that I say instead of saying hi."
He was, "*Yeah, I dig that,*
but you one of them weird cats,
who be sitting on prayer mats
meditating all day.
I wish I was like that
but I lost my way some time ago and ain't found it ever since."
I was like,
"There ain't no difference between me and you.
It's true I may hold another view
but we the same breed,
brother, we bleed the same things
and have the same needs.
Ain't none of us strong enough
to walk this path all alone.
And even the greatest of super heroes needs some saving at times."

"Well at this time,
I could care less wether I live or die.
Matter of fact I'm leaning more towards death.
I got no job, a baby on the way
and I'm facing my 3rd F.
25 with an L.
I might as well end it here.
My only fears be incarceration and failure.
I don't want my child to grow up with that psychological fatherless paraphernalia.
It happened to me.
I never knew my pops
he'd been locked down my entire life.
I figured all non-whites was indigenous to cell blocks.
My moms struggled to keep us well stocked.
I had to hustle to get my first pair of shell tops,
became a minimum wage slave as a bell hop.
Worked at the local Marriot.
I had to cater to the demands of old rich white people
who thought they were greater than me.
On some white supremacy,
superiority complex.
Saying, Nigga, do that!
Boy, grab this!
Got me vexed,
and one day I flexed on this old white dude.
It wasn't my fault

I got hit with armed robbery and aggravated assault.
When I never touched him.
I was completely innocent.
Still all my freedoms were suspended.
I got released after two years
without no incidents on the inside,
but once on that outside
that F on my record
stood out like a scarlet letter on my chest.
No one would hire me
because I was a potential liability.
Unemployment
I violated my probation
and got locked up again,
another disappointment.
Can you see this vicious cycle that's my life?
And I worked hard to do right.
To do things that legal way.
Then once again I got probation
and got a job as a mason
when I replied no felonies on my application,
but it was only a matter of time
before they found out.
Background check
got released
but they said they wouldn't tell the police that I lied.
And for months I tried everything
but playa, there were no opportunities.
Let down my lady
who was the only one to ever be true to me.
With a baby on the way
the only feasible way for me to get paid
is to slang D,
but killing my own people to make a living don't make no sense to me.
I guess I got a conscience, right?
I would move but I ain't got no funds,
so I'm forced to rot here
under this California sun.
When I was young
I was told the streets here were paved in gold,
and the sky is the limit,
but now i'm looking to end it
in this frigid pacific ocean.
Here's my white flag I surrender,
tell the white man he's the victor again.
And I apologize to my sisters, my family and my friends,
especially to my lady and my unborn child."

And then he paused a while,

I let it sink in
and started thinking
like what would I do if I was him.
If things had gone contrary to what I expected.
Instead of driving by,
if that cop stopped, beat me down and had me arrested.
If one of my parents died
or if I was denied a chance to go to school.
Would I be who I am now?
And before I could answer that
he told me something that I would never forget
as long as I live.

"Man, I figured by now you'd be able to tell,
but I guess I overestimated you
expected you
to understand this tale
that's my life.
But can't you tell, that I'm just you under a different light?
And if they ask you who it was that died here tonight
please, make sure that they say my name right.
You know it's pronounced Ty-son."

Ty-son, what you saying you me?
Ty-son, nah, homie you can't be.

Who would you be if things in your life had gone differently?
If this game dealt you a hand that you couldn't handle?
Went from rags to riches,
from fame to struggling.
Your life is precious, but what are you really coveting?
Take a walk in someone else's shoes and experience their life

Who would you be under a different light?
Who would you be under a different light?
Who would you be under a different light?

Vocabulary Study Chart: "Under a Different Light"

Word	Definition(s) and Synonym(s)	Copy the line or sentence from the text.	Your own example sentence
Hypothesis			
Salutation			
Paraphernalia			
Conscience			

Word	Definition(s) and Synonym(s)	Copy the line or sentence from the text.	Your own example sentence
Prestige			
Myriad			
Actualize			
Extricating			
Divergent			

Word	Definition(s) and Synonym(s)	Copy the line or sentence from the text.	Your own example sentence
Imperceptible			
Pejorative			
Definitive			

Black Boy Poems Analytical Learning Experience

In the poem *"Under a Different Light"* a reference is made to the book the *Scarlett Letter* by Nathaniel Hawthorne. The line from the poem is, "that F on my record stood out like a scarlet letter on my chest." The focus of this LE is to compare and contrast the experiences of the protagonist in the *Scarlet Letter* with the protagonist in *Under a Different Light*.

Hester Prynne from *Scarlet Letter*

Who is she?

What did she do?

What is a Scarlet Letter? What was the purpose of the Scarlet Letter? How does one receive a Scarlet Letter in her society?

What were the consequences she experienced as a result of the Scarlet Letter?

What institutions in society were responsible for enforcing the rules and consequences of the Scarlett Letter? What are the demographics of those institutions? Do you feel they had a bias in how they enforced their rules and consequences. Explain.

Do you believe she would've been treated differently if she had been a man in that society? Explain your answer.

Character 2 from Under a Different Light

Who is he?

What is his scarlet letter? What was the cause of his scarlet letter?

What were the consequences he experienced as a result of his scarlet letter?

What institutions in society were responsible for enforcing the rules and consequences of Character 2's scarlet letter? What are the demographics of those institutions? Do you feel they had a bias in how they enforced their rules and consequences. Explain.

How would Character 2 be treated differently if he was a white man, wealthy or in possession of some other "privilege" in society? How would he have been treated differently if he belonged to some other disenfranchised group in society? Explain.

Can you think of any people in your family or community that wear scarlet letters? What needs to change in order for their lives to be different/better, for them to not face the institutional stigma of being branded with that scarlet letter?

What other people or groups in our society today do you feel are receiving the scarlet letter treatment? Describe who they are and explain why you think they receive this treatment?

Do you believe you have been branded with a scarlet letter by your society? Explain what letter, and why you feel you've been branded with this letter.

Possible resources for Scarlet Letter

https://www.youtube.com/watch?v=uen92KjCSsg

https://www.youtube.com/watch?v=aktGDEZTYYk

Black Boy Poems Research Learning Experience

In the poem "Under a Different Light" the science fiction motif (theme) of meeting an alternate version of oneself is used. This allowed Tyson to explore other possible life outcomes based on the conditions he lived in. The goal of this LE is for learners to become more familiar with the "statistical life chances" of their contemporaries/classmates from other ethnic, cultural, geographic and social/political backgrounds.

Life expectancy

Education

Health

Experience in school

Contact with law

Juvenile

jail/prison

Employment

Housing

Wealth

Trauma

Figure out the demographics for your state, city and school. Collect the statistics for members of those groups and compare them with the statistics that represent your demographic. Create a chart that allows you to compare your numbers with members of other communities.

Critical Analysis Questions

Do you feel our society should treat people differently because of how they are "defined" by some demographic marker? Explain.

What did you learn based on the different statistical life chances for your contemporaries? What groups have the "best" and "worst" statistical life chances?

What factors in our society do you feel contribute to creating these results?

How do you feel about the inequity between the different community experiences? Explain. What concrete steps can be taken to make systemic change to create a more equitable society?

Black Boy Poems Curriculum

"Dream Revisited"

Dream Revisited

I wrote this to challenge the false framing of Dr. King in this moment of August of 1963. As if, he did not do anything else after the fact, and that this one moment was his most important accomplishment. I also wrote it to bring Dr. King of 1963 up to date on things that have transpired throughout the black community and the world since his speech. I think this can be a powerful way of introducing learners to interacting with historical texts. We can understand and appreciate the text in its historical context. We can also take it further and interact with it utilizing the lessons we've learned from history up until the present moment.

Themes:

- Interacting/Responding to historical text. (Giving the learners a platform to engage with a text, think critically about it and analyze it through a historic and contemporary lens.

- Dr. King's I Have A Dream Speech

- Civil Rights Movement

- Problems in the USA during the 50s and 60s.

Prerequisites and Scaffolding:

-Analysis in context. Analyzing something in the temporal context that produced it. Then analyzing it through the lens of a contemporary context.

I make a number of references that the learners might not be familiar with:

-Agent Orange
-Gulf War syndrome
-Bull Connor
-Mark Fuhrman
-Audubon Ball Room
-Bo Jangles
-Blackface
-Buckwheat (from the Little Rascals)
-16th Street Church Bombing (4 Little Girls)
-Smack (slang for heroine)
-3rd strike for stealing a slice of pizza
-White Hyundai (Rodney King)
-Dreaming in your car (Tyisha Miller)

Implementation of Curriculum:

1. Initial Poem Reflection Learning Experience

2. Vocabulary Learning Experience

3. Second Poem Reflection Learning Experience

4. Unique Learning Experiences: Dream Revisited

This section has one official unique LE and one extra LE that could be used as a prerequisite LE.

How would you update Dr. King:

This LE is asking learners to do the same thing I attempted to do with my poem. As of 2019 we are 56 years post the *I Have A Dream* speech. This LE is asking learners to use what they know of the world around them to speak to whether or not Dr. King's dream has manifested in our society. It also asks them to craft a message that would update Dr. King on the world today.

This is one of the first LEs that is really pushing the students to use their critical analysis abilities to focus on what they see when they look at the world, and then tying it to King's historical statement being made in the context of 1963.

Second LE

You could use this to help the learners gain a better understanding of the historical references I made in the poem. It might be a great way to actually begin the LEs for this chapter. It would give them more context when they watch/listen to the poem.

5. Deep Dive Poetry Analysis/Literary Device Learning Experience

6. Chapter Review Learning Experience

Expansion LEs:

Compare and contrast King's focus in the I have A Dream Speech with his

Beyond Vietnam and The Other America speeches.
Dream Revisited

Chronological and Spatial Thinking

Students compare the present with the past, evaluating the consequences of past events and decisions and determining the lessons that were learned.

Students analyze how change happens at different rates at different times; understand that some aspects can change while others remain the same; and understand that change is complicated and affects not only technology and politics but also values and beliefs.

Historical Research, Evidence, and Point of View

Students identify bias and prejudice in historical interpretations.

Students evaluate major debates among historians concerning alternative interpretations of the past, including an analysis of authors' use of evidence and the distinctions between sound generalizations and misleading oversimplifications.

Students construct and test hypotheses; collect, evaluate, and employ information from multiple primary and secondary sources; and apply it in oral and written presentations.

Historical Interpretation

Students show the connections, causal and otherwise, between particular historical events and larger social, economic, and political trends and developments.

Students recognize the complexity of historical causes and effects, including the limitations on determining cause and effect.

Students interpret past events and issues within the context in which an event unfolded rather than solely in terms of present-day norms and values.

Students understand the meaning, implication, and impact of historical events and recognize that events could have taken other directions.

Standards and Learning objectives

4. Examine the roles of civil rights advocates (e.g., A. Philip Randolph, Martin Luther King, Jr., Malcom X, Thurgood Marshall, James Farmer, Rosa Parks), including the significance of Martin Luther King, Jr.'s "Letter from Birmingham Jail" and "I Have a Dream" speech.

Discuss the diffusion of the civil rights movement of African Americans from the churches of the rural South and the urban North, including the resistance to racial desegregation in Little Rock and Birmingham, and how the advances influenced the agendas, strategies, and effectiveness of the quests of American Indians, Asian Americans, and Hispanic Americans for civil rights and equal opportunities.

6. Analyze the passage and effects of civil rights and voting rights legislation (e.g., 1964 Civil Rights Act, Voting Rights Act of 1965) and the Twenty-Fourth Amendment, with an emphasis on equality of access to education and to the political process.

Trace the origins and geopolitical consequences (foreign and domestic) of the Cold War and containment policy, including the following:

• The Vietnam War

Dream Revisited (2001)

You want to know my dreams?
I sleep to the sounds of M-16s,
because mostly blacks and browns died on the front-lines of Viet-Nam.
Inhale aromas of
napalm
and carpet bombs
through my lungs
and exhale screams of Viet-Cong
in a language foreign to my native tongue.
Agent Orange burns
my chromosomes like
Gulf War syndrome.
Putting holes in my girl's ovaries.
Babies born deformed
my words form this ghetto poetry.
And many nights I was torn from rest
like those police dogs who tore my flesh,
muscle from bone.

For freedom,
we marched determined
but Bull Conors and Mark Fuhrmans
turn on little innocent children
that powerful firehose.
Now my dreams consist of buildings named
Audubon
where bullets rip through my torso.
Like El Hajj Malik El Shabazz,
Malcolm X.
With stretch marks on my neck,
lynched, hung.
Under a southern sun.
They cut my penis off
because they into them phallic symbols.
And I sweat profusely in my sleep
because even in my dreams
I have to stay on my toes.
Nimble like
Bo Jangles,
Bo Jackson.
So now we
shuffle,
shuck,
 jive
to stay alive in black cleats
as athletes,

or in black face
with buck teeth
like buckwheat.
You see these types be stereo,
so they surround me like sound.
Y'all we victims of these terrible scenarios,
and some of us lose faith.
Which is one of the signs of this crazy world,
where we don't go to the mosque
or to the church no more
because that's where they blew up
4 little girls.
And many nights I had to make the street my pillow,
it's where I dream dreams of poverty and skin disease,
because eczema
covers my epidermis.
From shooting smack in HIV infected
hypodermic needles.
Convulsions in a fetal position
in the back of a dark alley.
As that poison kills parts of my cerebral cortex,
because we already dead to them more or less.
So in my dreams
my children play with death.
Some smoke sess and
drink liquid death and
pack weapons of death on their waistlines.
Capable of causing an instant flatline.
Them tech-9s and latest designs
of high powered weaponry.
I think you can see
these dreams
ain't no friend of mine.
Because in most dreams ya'll I'm claustrophobic.
Chained in the belly of slave ships
with my brothers and sisters.
Or confined by walls,
cells
6 by 9.
Doing time
25 to life
because my third strike
was theft of a slice of pizza.
Ay, yo, Judge
I was hoping you could see I'm just a hungry child on welfare.
With these crazy dreams of being a fresh prince of Bel Air.
But now I'm the prince of a cell with mildew and stale air.
Where a white guard will come escort me to a court yard
where I get to see the sun

for only 1 hour a day,
and then back to lock up.
But you see this brother named Nas
he told me with words like this,
"I never sleep because sleep is the cousin of death."
I'm trying to take that advice because this sleep ain't nothing nice.
Because in my dream sleep
is where zombies of fiends speak.
And I walk with bodies riddled by bullets because of these mean streets.
Where the demon police
will leave you bleeding for speeding in a white Hyundai,
and on the wrong day
if you dreaming in your car
and they wake you up with guns drawn
and you respond the wrong way,
it's bombs away.
Bullet holes in driver side windows and doors,
but the thing be
is these dreams are metaphors.
Reflections
of what I see in my 24-7
the suffering,
the oppression,
the poverty,
the depression,
the hustling
without resting,
these are my realities without question.
And when I rest my head at night
you see my dreams
manifest them.

Vocabulary Study Chart: "Dream Revisited"

Word	Definition(s) and Synonym(s)	Copy the line or sentence from the text.	Your own example sentence
Viet-Cong			
Profusely			
Eczema			
Epidermis			

Word	Definition(s) and Synonym(s)	Copy the line or sentence from the text.	Your own example sentence
Claustrophobic			
Metaphors			
Manifest			
Inadequate			

Word	Definition(s) and Synonym(s)	Copy the line or sentence from the text.	Your own example sentence
Accommodations			

Black Boy Poems Writing Learning Experience

"Dream Revisited" was written as a response to Dr. Martin Luther King Jr.'s "I Have a Dream" speech (1963). The author, Tyson Amir, was attempting to inform the Dr. King of 1963 about things that have transpired in various communities throughout the world since his famous speech. In this LE you will do the same thing that Tyson attempted to do.

1. Read/Listen/Watch Dr. Martin Luther King Jr.'s "I Have a Dream" speech and summarize its main points.

2. In your opinion, what was his dream for society? Do you believe it was a good dream for our society? Explain. Do you feel our society has accomplished any of that dream? Explain your answer.

3. Summarize the main points of Tyson Amir's "Dream Revisited." What were the major ideas he was attempting to bring to Dr. King's attention? What are some of the points in the poem that demonstrate that Dr. King's vision had not become a reality at the time the poem was written?

4. How would you update Dr. King on the state of affairs in the world today in relation to his dream?

Black Boy Poems Research Learning Experience

In the poem "Dream Revisited" a number of social, cultural, political and historical references are made. The goal of this LE is to make learners more familiar with these references and their context.

Context:

Dream Revisited was written as a response to Dr. Martin Luther King Jr.'s I Have a Dream speech. Which was given in August of 1963. Tyson was attempting to update the Dr. King of 1963 on things that have transpired in various communities throughout the world since the famous speech.

Method:

Research each of these references in the poem

1. Vietnam War and combat/death by color

2. Agent Orange (Vietnam)

3. Gulf War Syndrome

4. Police dogs used on non-violent civil rights protesters

5. Bull Connor

6. Mark Fuhrman

7. Audubon Ballroom (New York)

8. Lynchings of Black people and other people of color in the 1900s

9. Bo Jangles

10. Black Face

11. Buckwheat (Character)

12. Birmingham Church Bombing

Review Questions

1. Are there any individuals or groups of people currently in society who are working to make a reality of Dr. King's dream? If so, then who are they and what work are they doing. What aspects of Dr. King's dream are they focusing on?

2. What major issues in today's society align with issues that Dr. King was highlighting in his speech?

3. How do you feel Dr. King would react to the current social, political and economic climate in our society today? Explain.

4. Based on your findings from the research from page 1 of this LE, how many contemporary parallels can you find for those historic references Tyson Amir made in the poem "Dream Revisited"? List the historic reference and contemporary reference side by side.

"Between Huey and Malcolm"

Between Huey and Malcolm

I believe this piece is the strongest example of social/political commentary and critique in the book. It's a very raw piece. It is filled rich language drawn from a variety of historical and contemporary sources. There's quite a few literary devices and techniques spread throughout the poem.

A little background on the title of the poem, my original writing is placed between two historic quotes that begin and end the poem. Making this another poem that interacts with historic literature, and giving the title a literal and figurative meaning.

Themes:

- Media stereotypes. The poem begins with a quote by Dr. Huey P. Newton talking about representation in media. The piece then goes on to highlight specific instances of media stereotypes and bias.

- Cannibalism (I make a number of references to how the society is feasting on black bodies in multiple ways)

- Pop culture references (I used a number of movies and television shows to help tell the story in the poem. Pan's Labyrinth, 3rd Rock From the Sun, Malcolm in the Middle, Third Watch and The Walking Dead)

Prerequisites and Scaffolding:

For this chapter the learners would really benefit from having an opportunity to learn more about some of the historical references I make in the poem.

- Mike Vick's case and prison sentence.
- George Zimmerman's case and court experience.
- Walter Scott
- Eric Garner
- Oscar Grant
- Significance of four score and seven years ago
- Bell Curve (the book by Charles Murray and Richard Herrnstein and its claim of IQ differences based on "race". And of course black people according to "research" are genetically predisposed to have lower IQs)
- Intelligent quotient (IQ tests, their historic bias and racist application)
- Robert Kirkman (The creator of The Walking Dead)
- Rachel Dolezal
- Huey P. Newton received his Ph.D. from UC Santa Cruz

Implementation of Curriculum:

1. Initial Poem Reflection Learning Experience

2. Vocabulary Learning Experience

3. Second Poem Reflection Learning Experience

4. Unique Learning Experiences: Between Huey and Malcolm

This section has three LEs.

The first two allow the learners to do some research on Dr. Huey P. Newton and Malcolm X. Feel free to have the learners write down the responses to their research on the document. If they need more space for their responses, then they can write on another sheet of paper or on a computer/tablet.

COINTELPRO

The third LE asks the learners to engage with a very import primary source document. The FBI's COINTELPRO memo of 3/4/1968. The LE asks the learners to respond to each of the five points in the document and use their critical thinking skills to reflect on the document's significance historically and presently.

5. Deep Dive Poetry Analysis/Literary Device Learning Experience

6. Chapter Review Learning Experience

Expansion LEs:

- By Any Means Necessary speech (Malcolm X)

- Analysis of the 10 Point Platform and Program (Black Panther Party)

- The impact of the BPP's free breakfast for children program.

- Other groups that were heavily surveilled by the federal government. And what were the reasonings for their surveillance.

- What groups are being surveilled today?

- The Technology Question by Dr. Huey P. Newton

- Intercommunalism (Theory created by Dr. Huey P. Newton)

- The alliance the BPP had with the LGBTQ community and other groups.

Between Huey and Malcolm

Chronological and Spatial Thinking

Students compare the present with the past, evaluating the consequences of past events and decisions and determining the lessons that were learned.

Students analyze how change happens at different rates at different times; understand that some aspects can change while others remain the same; and understand that change is complicated and affects not only technology and politics but also values and beliefs.

Historical Research, Evidence, and Point of View

Students distinguish valid arguments from fallacious arguments in historical interpretations.

Students identify bias and prejudice in historical interpretations.

Students construct and test hypotheses; collect, evaluate, and employ information from multiple primary and secondary sources; and apply it in oral and written presentations.

Historical Interpretation

Students show the connections, causal and otherwise, between particular historical events and larger social, economic, and political trends and developments.

Students recognize the complexity of historical causes and effects, including the limitations on determining cause and effect.

Students interpret past events and issues within the context in which an event unfolded rather than solely in terms of present-day norms and values.

Students understand the meaning, implication, and impact of historical events and recognize that events could have taken other directions.

Standards and Learning objectives

7. Understand the functions and responsibilities of a free press.

Students evaluate and take and defend positions on the influence of the media on American political life.

1. Discuss the meaning and importance of a free and responsible press.

2. Describe the roles of broadcast, print, and electronic media, including the Internet, as means of communication in American politics.

3. Explain how public officials use the media to communicate with the citizenry and to shape public opinion.

5. Understand the Thirteenth, Fourteenth, and Fifteenth Amendments to the Constitution and analyze their connection to Reconstruction.

3. Explain imperialism from the perspective of the colonizers and the colonized and the varied immediate and long-term responses by the people under colonial rule.

4. Describe the independence struggles of the colonized regions of the world, including the roles of leaders, such as Sun Yat-sen in China, and the roles of ideology and religion.

Between Huey And Malcolm (2015)

Dr. Huey P. Newton had an epiphany and then said, "I don't expect the white media to create positive black male images."

So he wouldn't be surprised to see how
evening networks
accumulate their net worth
of billions
off assassinating the character of our children.
They "objectively" report the news about black lives,
matter
of factly
they spin white lies
that evolve into black lies
about black lives
because we don't matter to them
only in terms of
their bottom line.

You see our worth in their eyes
is somewhere between
feline and pigeon.
Y'all, we still less than k-9s.
Because ninjas remember how they sent that boy Mike Vick to prison,
but be the color of George Zimmerman,
a private citizen,
and you can legally murder a nigga
and walk off Scott free.
But Walter Scott can't flee,
and Eric Garner can't breathe,
Tyisha Miller can't sleep,
and Oscar Grant can't see his daughter no more.
Oh no, this ain't no folklore.
This is so much more.
Four score and 7 years ago
nah, before that.
1619
the first time them white beings
brought us to these shores,
and since then
it's been
all
out
war.

You see their strategies and tactics have adapted.
They went from De Jure to De Facto,

ipso facto,
they've tormented and attacked us
to extinguish the light of black souls.
Theirs is a pathological praxis.
Rooted in a xenophobic,
schizophrenic,
racially insecure
culturally immature social apparatus.
Which forces them to concoct a reality
that confers to them an unearned status
of unmerited advantage.
To make them feel adequate.
In turn
we are termed
the thugs and the savages.
Whole deck stacked against us
we victims of Bell Curves,
Intelligent Quotient averages.
Recipients of jail terms,
we residents of these ghetto pan's labyrinths.
And very few of us can survive the madness.
And for those that do
them government issued bullets
fly faster than light travels from the sun to our planet.
That 3rd Rock from the Sun.
They trying to have me Malcolm in the Middle,
nah, I'm Malcolm in the window
on Third Watch
watching over our daughters and sons.
Kalashnikov 47 cocked for them when they come,
and we know
they gonna come.
Because for us,
this land is a Robert Kirkman graphic novel,
for it feeds off the blood of our young.

We

are

The Walking Dead.

Just channeling our inner Tyrese
because we ain't destined to make it passed
the first few letter boxes of the first few sheets.

We

are

akin to proteins and fatty lipids in the belly of the beast.
Our appendages
are the meat of fleshy mangoes
stuck in teeth.
To be plucked and sucked in
moments after the feast.

Now let that digest.

Yeah, I know these words hit hard to the gut like dysentery.
Or hard to the brain
like religious missionaries colonizing souls and minds.
No matter how you reduce it,
pain is the protocol.
You either die or revoke your past
or try to pass as something you're not
on that Rachel Dolezal.
But, ya'll, we can't opt out.
We can't drop out.
Especially when them cops is out.
That index itchy when them guns come out.
We go to sleep dreaming at night wishing it would all run out
and be replaced by something different when the sun comes out.
But day breaks
and the morning is here,
and we find ourselves in mourning again.
And I don't want to see
anymore mornings
where we mourning kith and kin.
So I guess that means
that we're back on that Malcolm again.

In essence it only means we want one thing.
We declare our right on this earth to be a man,
to be a human being,
to be respected as a human being,
to be given the rights of a human being
in this society,
on this earth,
in this day,
which we intend to bring
into existence by any means necessary!

Vocabulary Study Chart: "Between Huey and Malcolm"

Word	Definition(s) and Synonym(s)	Copy the line or sentence from the text.	Your own example sentence
Epiphany			
Accumulate			
Folklore			
De Jure			

Word	Definition(s) and Synonym(s)	Copy the line or sentence from the text.	Your own example sentence
De Facto			
Ipso Facto			
Pathological			
Praxis			

Word	Definition(s) and Synonym(s)	Copy the line or sentence from the text.	Your own example sentence
Xenophobic			
Confer			
Appendages			
Dysentery			

Word	Definition(s) and Synonym(s)	Copy the line or sentence from the text.	Your own example sentence
Protocol			
Inoculate			
Kith and Kin			

Black Boy Poems Research Learning Experience

In the poem Between Huey and Malcolm the piece begins with a quote from Dr. Huey P. Newton and ends with a quote from Malcolm X. Both Huey and Malcolm are very important historical and revolutionary figures with important legacies. The focus of this LE is to become more familiar with the life work of both of these figures.

Dr. Huey P. Newton

Who was Huey P. Newton?

Where was he raised? What was his school experience like?

How did he become educated?

What was his cause? What did he stand for? Explain

What organization(s) was he affiliated with? When did they start, and what were their goals?

What did he accomplish, and what did his organization(s) accomplish? What's his legacy?

Black Boy Poems Research Learning Experience

In the poem Between Huey and Malcolm the piece begins with a quote from Dr. Huey P. Newton and ends with a quote from Malcolm X. Both Huey and Malcolm are very important historical and revolutionary figures with important legacies. The focus of this LE is to become more familiar with the life work of both of these figures.

Malcolm X

Who was Malcolm X?

Where was he raised? What was his school experience like?

How did he become educated?

What was his cause? What did he stand for? Explain

What organization(s) was he affiliated with? When did they start, and what were their goals?

What did he accomplish, and what did his organization(s) accomplish? What's his legacy?

Black Boy Poems Writing Learning Experience

Both Dr. Huey P. Newton and Malcolm X were targets of US government surveillance campaigns. Arguably the most famous program of the 20th century was the FBI's COINTELPRO (Counter Intelligence Program). This was directed by the head of the FBI J. Edgar Hoover. COINTELPRO surveilled multiple groups from various communities but used the majority of its resources to surveil black political organizations. The goal of this LE is to allow learners to become more familiar with the strategies and tactics of the US federal government's COINTELPRO.

On March 4, 1968 the FBI published a very important document which launched one of the most destructive government campaigns in the history of this country. Many of us have never heard of COINTELPRO but we have suffered the consequences. Explain your reactions below to each point of the Counter Intelligence Program 3/4/68 memo.

Point 1. What are your thoughts and feelings? Why do you think they began with this point? What is the FBI focused on preventing and why?

Point 2. What is significant to you about this point? How does point 2 relate to point 1? Why do you feel the FBI would make this such a high priority?

Point 3. What is significant about this point? How do you feel you've seen the reality of this point play out in our society? What is the connection between the date of this memo and one of the names mentioned in Point 2 of this document?

Point 4. Why is this point such an important strategy for those in power? Why do you feel the government focused on these 3 main groups? What are some ways that you feel this point might have been actualized during the late 60s?

Point 5. The majority of you working on this LE would be considered youth. For those who are not, you most likely have children or young people under you that you care about. How do you feel about the government specifically targeting youth? Explain. In what ways do you feel you've been able to witness the impact of this point in your life? Explain.

What thoughts and feelings do you have about this document, COINTELPRO and this history? According to today's version of the FBI, what is a Black Identity Extremist? Do you feel there a similarities between what the FBI is saying now about Black Identity Extremists and COINTELPRO? Explain.

How does the US government reconcile its surveillance and infiltration of individuals and organizations when people are/were observing their constitutional rights? (1st, 2nd, 4th and 14th amendment rights) In what ways should those rights protect citizens from incursions by the government?

What other individuals and groups were being targeted by COINTELPRO? What other groups and individuals are current targets of government surveillance? Why are they being targeted?

GOALS
~~~~~

For maximum effectiveness of the Counterintelligence Program, and to prevent wasted effort, long-range goals are being set.

1.   Prevent the COALITION of militant black nationalist groups. In unity there is strength; a truism that is no less valid for all its triteness. An effective coalition of black nationalist groups might be the first step toward a real "Mau Mau" [Black revolutionary army] in America, the beginning of a true black revolution.

2.   Prevent the RISE OF A "MESSIAH" who could unify, and electrify, the militant black nationalist movement. Malcolm X might have been such a "messiah;" he is the martyr of the movement today. Martin Luther King, Stokely Carmichael and Elijah Muhammed all aspire to this position. Elijah Muhammed is less of a threat because of his age. King could be a very real contender for this position should he abandon his supposed "obedience" to "white, liberal doctrines" (nonviolence) and embrace black nationalism. Carmichael has the necessary charisma to be a real threat in this way.

3.   Prevent VIOLENCE on the part of black nationalist groups. This is of primary importance, and is, of course, a goal of our investigative activity; it should also be a goal of the Counterintelligence Program to pinpoint potential troublemakers and neutralize them before they exercise their potential for violence.

4.   Prevent militant black nationalist groups and leaders from gaining RESPECTABILITY, by discrediting them to three separate segments of the community. The goal of discrediting black nationalists must be handled tactically in three ways. You must discredit those groups and individuals to, first, the responsible Negro community. Second, they must be discredited to the white community, both the responsible community and to "liberals" who have vestiges of sympathy for militant black nationalist [sic] simply because they are Negroes. Third, these groups must be discredited in the eyes of Negro radicals, the followers of the movement. This last area requires entirely different tactics from the first two. Publicity about violent tendencies and radical statements merely enhances black nationalists to the last group; it adds "respectability" in a different way.

5.   A final goal should be to prevent the long-range GROWTH of militant black organizations, especially among youth. Specific tactics to prevent these groups from converting young people must be developed. [...]

113

TARGETS
~~~~~~~

Primary targets of the Counterintelligence Program, Black
Nationalist-Hate Groups, should be the most violent and radical groups and
their leaders. We should emphasize those leaders and organizations that
are nationwide in scope and are most capable of disrupting this country.
These targets, members, and followers of the:

Student Nonviolent Coordinating Committee (SNCC)
Southern Christian Leadership Conference (SCLC)
Revolutionary Action Movement (RAM)
NATION OF ISLAM (NOI)   [emphasis added]

Offices handling these cases and those of Stokely Carmichael of SNCC,
H. Rap Brown of SNCC, Martin Luther King of SCLC, Maxwell Stanford of RAM,
and Elijah Muhammed of NOI, should be alert for counterintelligence
suggestions. [...]

Black Boy Poems Curriculum

"Out"

Out

Out is another narrative based piece in the text. It's a composite of multiple experiences all stemming from a similar context. I synthesized the experiences and developed a general story that spoke to the individual experiences in a unified way. The piece also features a creative use of repetition to reinforce the central theme in the story.

Themes:

-Breaking the cycle. (How do we begin to break cycles or pattern that aren't beneficial)

-Unfair conditions that develop into systemic restrictions on life possibilities.

-Power of repetition, especially contextual repetition.

I've never counted how many times I've used the word out in the piece but the context shifts in almost ever usage. It's a clever literary technique but more importantly drives home the point of getting out.

-Composite/collage (how to create one narrative from multiple stories)

Prerequisites and Scaffolding:

- The reality of incarceration in the USA in comparison with our countries.

- The experiences of black people and other people of color in the prison industrial complex and criminal justice system.

- Social roles/social stratification (the ways in which our society is divided up to create roles. The way people are treated because of these roles. Race, Class, Caste, Religion, Gender, Sexual Orientation, Place of Origin, Language…)

Curriculum Implementation:

1. Initial Poem Reflection Learning Experience

2. Vocabulary Learning Experience

3. Second Poem Reflection Learning Experience

4. Unique Learning Experiences: Out

This chapter has two LEs.

This first is the Power Dynamic LE. This asks the learners to analyze "power" in our current society. Who has power? Who doesn't have power? What is the source of that power? How has power changed hands historically?

The questions will allow the learners to contextualize societal power dynamics and begin thinking about how those dynamics can be affected.

The second LE for this section is a Self Inventory LE. Learners are asked to think critically about the roles they see people playing around them in society. They're also asked to consider where the roles come from, and what role(s) they believe they'll be pressured to play.

5. Deep Dive Poetry Analysis/Literary Device Learning Experience

6. Chapter Review Learning Experience

Expansion LEs:

History of Jails and Prisons in the United States

Emergence of privatized prisons

The role of prisons in immigration

Out

Chronological and Spatial Thinking

Students compare the present with the past, evaluating the consequences of past events and decisions and determining the lessons that were learned.

Students analyze how change happens at different rates at different times; understand that some aspects can change while others remain the same; and understand that change is complicated and affects not only technology and politics but also values and beliefs.

Historical Research, Evidence, and Point of View

Students distinguish valid arguments from fallacious arguments in historical interpretations.

Students identify bias and prejudice in historical interpretations.

Students evaluate major debates among historians concerning alternative interpretations of the past, including an analysis of authors' use of evidence and the distinctions between sound generalizations and misleading oversimplifications.

Students construct and test hypotheses; collect, evaluate, and employ information from multiple primary and secondary sources; and apply it in oral and written presentations.

Historical Interpretation

Students show the connections, causal and otherwise, between particular historical events and larger social, economic, and political trends and developments.

Students recognize the complexity of historical causes and effects, including the limitations on determining cause and effect.

Students interpret past events and issues within the context in which an event unfolded rather than solely in terms of present-day norms and values.

Students understand the meaning, implication, and impact of historical events and recognize that events could have taken other directions.

Standards and Learning objectives

6. Students conduct cost-benefit analyses and apply basic economic indicators to analyze the aggregate economic behavior of the U.S. economy.

Students analyze the multiple causes, key events, and complex consequences of the Civil War.

2. Trace the boundaries constituting the North and the South, the geographical differences between the two regions, and the differences between agrarians and industrialists.

3. Identify the constitutional issues posed by the doctrine of nullification and secession and the earliest origins of that doctrine.

4. Discuss Abraham Lincoln's presidency and his significant writings and speeches and their relationship to the Declaration of Independence, such as his "House Divided" speech (1858), Gettysburg Address (1863), Emancipation Proclamation (1863), and inaugural addresses (1861 and 1865).

Out (2005)

He was born out of wedlock.
In and out of the arms of his pop,
who was in and out of trouble until he got shot.
His moms, in between jobs,
she in and out of relationships.
He starts sliding in and out of the house quick.
At school lessons go in one ear out the other.
Outside his window he sits to watch the gangsters and hustlers,
jump in and out of new cars and new shoes.
That cash go in and out of their pockets to keep em looking brand-new.
He's just a youth,
easily influenced
so he's intrigued
by these cats with no job
getting the money without a degree.
So he
starts cutting classes,
then drops out of school.
Now his hands are in and out of his pockets
with rocks like them other dudes.
He's a pawn in this game that's hard to break out.
He hangs out on the block
as this new scene plays out.
The decision's laid out,
it's either you in or you out.
Without a doubt he jumps in
scene one fade out.

You see his momma is out of his life now,
because she's living right now.
She tells him to stop hustling
that's the same path your pop went down.
He can't hear her,
he blocks it out.
Back on the block where them cops is out.
They staking him out because now he's got clout.
An undercover approaches to buy,
he had a notion something was strange
but he ignored it because he's out of his mind.
He's drunk and he's high.
Product and paper exchange hands.
PD jump out of three gray vans with guns drawn.
He's told,
"hands out your pockets! Better keep them high!"
His mom's prophecy comes true
ain't no escaping this time.

He's now property of the state
and can't wait to get out.
But on the outside life doesn't wait
he finds out that his woman is late.
Another born out of wedlock
away from the arms of his pop,
who's going to spend the years of his son's life
behind the doors of the cellblock.
When will this nonsense stop?
y'all got to tell me
when will this nonsense stop.

His baby is getting older now
starting to crawl,
you see youngster out on the yard playing basketball.
You see him out
by the three point line busting his J
with no thought of changing his life when he gets out someday.
He can't seem to think outside of the box
or outside of his block.
He's preparing to spend his life in jail
or outlined in chalk.
Because on them streets
you're always outnumbered and outgunned.
Prison and death are the only logical outcomes.
But he's way out of control,
he's in and out of the hole.
Is he ever going to figure it out
and break out
this outlaw Scarface complex?
Meanwhile his son is without a father
who lives without a conscience.
Because it was
under developed
enveloped
by these hellish streets.
I just tell it how I see it,
some of y'all claim my words sound bleak.
I would prefer
if these stories never came out my mouth,
but I am going to speak to the madness
until my folks break out.
Break out!

Vocabulary Study Chart: "Out"

Word	Definition(s) and Synonym(s)	Copy the line or sentence from the text.	Your own example sentence
Wedlock			
Clout			
Outliers			
Proximity			

Word	Definition(s) and Synonym(s)	Copy the line or sentence from the text.	Your own example sentence
Typecast			
Albeit			
Marginalization			
Blaxploitation			

Word	Definition(s) and Synonym(s)	Copy the line or sentence from the text.	Your own example sentence
Conscripted			
Myopic			

Black Boy Poems Research Learning Experience

In the chapter for the poem "Out" Tyson Amir takes a critical look at the "roles" that we as people play in our society.

Power lesson

Power Dynamic Institutional Power

Think of a situation in life when you felt powerful. Describe the situation and what made you feel powerful?

Think of a situation in life when you didn't feel powerful. Describe the situation and what made you feel powerless?

Can you think of people in our society who are powerful and powerless? What are different kinds of power/vulnerabilities you can think of?

Based on all you responded to above, what is your definition of power?

Who are the people/institutions with power in our society? Be as descriptive as possible.

How did these people/institutions obtain their power?

How do these people/institutions exercise and preserve their power?

How do we experience those in power?

How have people been stripped of power in this society?

What are some characteristics of the cultures of people stripped of power?

In the last line of the poem Tyson says, "I would prefer if these stories never came out my mouth but I have to speak to this madness until my folks break out. Break out". In the spirit of breaking out and creating change can you think of three examples of when the power dynamics have been overthrown? How was it accomplished?

Black Boy Poems Research Learning Experience

In the chapter for the poem "Out" Tyson Amir takes a critical look at the "roles" that we as people play in our society.

What roles do you see people playing around you in your school setting and community?

Where do these roles come from? Who do these roles benefit? How are the people who are forced to play these roles benefitting from the roles they play?

Are the roles that we find ourselves playing/adopting true representations of who we are as individuals and people? Explain why.

Where do we learn who we are supposed to be in society? How are these roles taught and learned? Explain.

Which of these prescribed roles in our society do you feel you'll end up fulfilling? Explain. Is it a role that you want to play? Explain.

What does one do when their desires, wants and beliefs are not in congruence with the prescribed roles of their society?

How do you feel about these roles that people are forced to play in our society? Do you believe they are helping to create a more just and equitable society for all? Explain your answer.

"Blue Devil"

Blue Devil

Themes:

- Vivid language/Imagery I attempted to paint some of the pressure, tension and trauma of incarceration.

- First person experience of the pain and pressure of incarceration. I wrote it this way to challenge the view that some may hold of incarcerated people. I wanted people to see the impact that these inhumane environments can have on people.

- 13th amendment and it's legalization of slavery via incarceration.

Prerequisites and Scaffolding:

- The history of forced enslavement, the 13th amendment and the current carceral state.

- Innocence a commodity that's bought and sold (critique of how the wealthy are able to use their wealth to manipulate the justice system and poor people, especially poor black people are victimized by it the most)

- Parallels between chattel slavery and the prison industrial complex

Curriculum Implementation:

1. Initial Poem Reflection Learning Experience

2. Vocabulary Learning Experience

3. Second Poem Reflection Learning Experience

4. Unique Learning Experiences: Blue Devil

This chapter has two LEs.

The first LE examines the history of policing using Dr. Kappeler's research which is cited in the text. Learners will respond to questions based on their analysis of Dr. Kappeler's work.

Our second LE in this chapter takes a look at incarceration versus education locally and nationally. Learners will research the costs and impacts of incarceration and the costs and impact of education.

5. Deep Dive Poetry Analysis/Literary Device Learning Experience

6. Chapter Review Learning Experience

Expansion LEs:

Analysis of budgetary priorities in the USA

Analysis of other countries and their spending on education versus incarceration.

Blue Devil

Chronological and Spatial Thinking

Students compare the present with the past, evaluating the consequences of past events and decisions and determining the lessons that were learned.

Students analyze how change happens at different rates at different times; understand that some aspects can change while others remain the same; and understand that change is complicated and affects not only technology and politics but also values and beliefs.

Students relate current events to the physical and human characteristics of places and regions.

Historical Research, Evidence, and Point of View

Students distinguish valid arguments from fallacious arguments in historical interpretations.

Students identify bias and prejudice in historical interpretations.

Students evaluate major debates among historians concerning alternative interpretations of the past, including an analysis of authors' use of evidence and the distinctions between sound generalizations and misleading oversimplifications.

Students construct and test hypotheses; collect, evaluate, and employ information from multiple primary and secondary sources; and apply it in oral and written presentations.

Historical Interpretation

Students show the connections, causal and otherwise, between particular historical events and larger social, economic, and political trends and developments.

Students recognize the complexity of historical causes and effects, including the limitations on determining cause and effect.

Students interpret past events and issues within the context in which an event unfolded rather than solely in terms of present-day norms and values.

Students understand the meaning, implication, and impact of historical events and recognize that events could have taken other directions.

Standards and Learning objectives

5. Discuss Article III of the Constitution as it relates to judicial power, including the length of terms of judges and the jurisdiction of the Supreme Court.

Evaluate the major debates that occurred during the development of the Constitution and their ultimate resolutions in such areas as shared power among institutions, divided state-federal power, slavery, the rights of individuals and states (later addressed by the addition of the Bill of Rights), and the status of American Indian nations under the commerce clause.

2. Trace the origins and development of slavery; its effects on black Americans and on the region's political, social, religious, economic, and cultural development; and identify the strategies that were tried to both overturn and preserve it (e.g., through the writings and historical documents on Nat Turner, Denmark Vesey).

Blue Devil (2002)

Boxed in on all sides nowhere to run or to turn to
I box concrete walls until my hands turn blue.
Broken and swollen knuckles
skin torn and chapped,
I find freedom in syntax
that seeps through the cracks in the walls
to reach them cats
still on the outside.
How many years have I been on the inside?
I lost count.
Days become nights, weeks become years,
planets revolve around the sun
and I'm still stuck inside here.
Evolved into an animal
forgot what the world looked like.
Push-ups and sit-ups prepare me for fist fights.
They move me through the prison population cuffs fit my wrist tight.
I'm at my wits end because my bid is life.
Can you imagine being locked in a cage
for the rest of your days
plus some?
Surrounded by shadows and dark thoughts
of making my heart stop
with bad habits and odd customs.
I try to hang myself when the doors are locked
to make it stop.
But more of us get caught up everyday.
Over 2 million and counting.
From a bird's eye view
I have flashbacks of old days
how they carried us away from our homes
shackled in chains,
deja vu
because modern day prisoners are slaves.
Check your constitution
I ain't the first one to say it,
the prison industry is the new slave ship,
slave ship

Innocence a commodity that's bought and sold
but oddly escapes the possession of my black body.
I manifest Rodney King dreams
when I hear license and registration,
because reaching for my ID could be
justification for my homicide.
The wrong color at the wrong time.

You're a fool if you believe justice is colorblind.
In the belly of the beast on streets I stand
with hands cuffed behind my back
and get beat with black wood objects
in Oklahoma City
or smashed on hoods of squad cars in Inglewood projects.
Already walking with chains around my neck
they just ain't found a crime to convict me of yet.
Because as I speak
they framing crime scenes
to confine me
that's why what i'm rhyming about be pertinent
because police interaction be beyond permanent.
Pigs becoming judge, jury and executioner.
The majority of pigs are white
and this is why some might compare white folks to Lucifer.
For many this life be a living hell
so we rebel in these streets
screaming and yelling.
Product of environment
so therefore I'm a son of rebellion.

Vocabulary Study Chart: "Blue Devil"

Word	Definition(s) and Synonym(s)	Copy the line or sentence from the text.	Your own example sentence
Syntax			
Evolved			
Deja vu			
Commodity			

Word	Definition(s) and Synonym(s)	Copy the line or sentence from the text.	Your own example sentence
Manifest			
Pertinent			

Black Boy Poems Research Learning Experience

Written Response

"The birth and development of the American police can be traced to a multitude of historical, legal, and political-economic conditions. The institution of slavery and the control of minorities, however, were two of the more formidable historic features of American society shaping early policing. Slave patrols and Night Watches, which later became modern police departments, were both designed to control the behaviors of minorities …

"Blacks have long been targets of abuse. The use of patrols to capture runaway slaves was one of the precursors of formal police forces, especially in the South. This disastrous legacy persisted as an element of the police role even after the passage of the Civil Rights Act of 1964." - Victor E. Kappeler, Ph.D."

According to Dr. Victor E. Kappeler where is the birth and origin of American policing found?

What were two of the predecessor formations that eventually led to "police?"

Were you familiar with this history? How does this history of policing make you feel? Explain. What history of the "police" are you familiar with, and what have you been told about the purpose and function of law enforcement agencies in today's society? Explain.

In light of this history and the common notion of law enforcement agents as servants and protectors, who were the early iterations of police serving and protecting? Who became their primary targets? Do you believe it is possible for an organization so deeply rooted in racist history and institutional practices to ever fully shed its racist past and "serve and protect" everyone equally? Explain.

Read Dr. Kappeler's article entitled A Brief History of Slavery and the Origins of American Policing. Write down your responses to the history covered in Dr. Kappeler's article.

Black Boy Poems Research Learning Experience

But more of us get caught up everyday, over 2 million and counting, from a bird's eye view I have flashbacks of old days how they carried us away from our home shackled and chained, deja vu because modern day prisoners are slaves. Check your constitution I ain't the first one to say it. The prison industry is the new slave ship. - Blue Devil

They spend more on prison than school to imprison me in my surroundings. - Cali Story

The United States is currently in a public education climate that is sometimes described as the school to prison pipeline. Meaning that certain students are pushed from schools into jails and prisons. (ACLU)

What does education mean to you personally and within your family?

What significance does education have within your society?

How does a society benefit from well educated people? How does a society benefit from poorly educated people? Explain.

How much money do you think is spent on every student in your school?

How much money is spent on each student in your school? (Research)

How much money do you think is spent on each person incarcerated in jail and prison?

How much money is spent on each person incarcerated in jail and prison in your state? (Research)

Where is the closest jail or prison that is privately owned in your area? Who owns it and how much money do they make a year off incarceration?

What is the price of tuition for the closest community college, state college and private college in your area?

What is the average cost that a student pays for a four year college education? What is the average amount of debt a college graduate owes?

What are the current unemployment rates based on race and gender in the United States? What are the current unemployment rates for college graduates based on race and gender?

Compare your state's budget for education with its budget for incarceration. List those numbers. Do you believe investing more in quality education over incarceration is better for a society? Explain your answer.

Black Boy Poems Curriculum

"War Zones"

War Zones

Themes:

- Metaphor - the entire song can be viewed as a metaphor.

- The concept of home. What is home when you've been forced to move to another land? The experience of a people when their "home" wages war on them. What is home when your "home" now deems you "illegal" or concocts some other reason for denying your rights and claims to home?

- Resistance. When is it the right time to resist? How have people resisted? What is "just" resistance?

Prerequisites and Scaffolding:

- The story of Arjuna in the *Baghavad Gita*. This also provides an opportunity to introduce more context for Indian historical, religious and cultural traditions.

- *Things Fall Apart* by Chinua Achebe is an example of a text that parallels the central conflict in War Zones. There are other texts that could be used to help illustrate how a people respond to an imperial/colonial power taking over their land.

- Apartheid Struggle

- Jim Crow

Curriculum Implementation:

1. Initial Poem Reflection Learning Experience

2. Vocabulary Learning Experience

3. Second Poem Reflection Learning Experience

4. Unique Learning Experiences: War Zones

This chapter has one unique LE.

In the essay for the chapter War Zones I say, "All those who answer the call to arms have become Arjuna in the "Bhagavad Gita." We are a princely warrior caste, and we must do our dharma, which is to fight because our home has declared war upon us due to the color of our skin. The black child is born into a war zone, where he/she is destined to live and die."

In this LE the learners will learn more about the story of Arjuna and explore the parallels between his fight and some of the historic and contemporary struggles today. This LE provided an opportunity to engage with texts outside of the western canon and demonstrate ways in which learners can pull lessons from other cultures that can help them better understand themselves and the world around them.

5. Deep Dive Poetry Analysis/Literary Device Learning Experience

6. Chapter Review Learning Experience

Expansion LEs:

Finding other historical examples of times and places where a people's home becomes their war zone. Analyzing the ways in which those people responded to that situation.

Context, conditions, causes, and consequences. The learners might find quite a few examples that are results of colonization. This is a great way for learners to see parallels between the struggles of other peoples throughout the world.

War Zones

Chronological and Spatial Thinking

Students compare the present with the past, evaluating the consequences of past events and decisions and determining the lessons that were learned.

Students analyze how change happens at different rates at different times; understand that some aspects can change while others remain the same; and understand that change is complicated and affects not only technology and politics but also values and beliefs.

Historical Research, Evidence, and Point of View

Students construct and test hypotheses; collect, evaluate, and employ information from multiple primary and secondary sources; and apply it in oral and written presentations.

Historical Interpretation

Students show the connections, causal and otherwise, between particular historical events and larger social, economic, and political trends and developments.

Students recognize the complexity of historical causes and effects, including the limitations on determining cause and effect.

Students interpret past events and issues within the context in which an event unfolded rather than solely in terms of present-day norms and values.

Students understand the meaning, implication, and impact of historical events and recognize that events could have taken other directions.

Standards and Learning objectives

3. Understand the effects of the Freedmen's Bureau and the restrictions placed on the rights and opportunities of freedmen, including racial segregation and "Jim Crow" laws.

12.10 Students formulate questions about and defend their analyses of tensions within our constitutional democracy and the importance of maintaining a balance between the following concepts: majority rule and individual rights; liberty and equality; state and national authority in a federal system; civil disobedience and the rule of law; freedom of the press and the right to a fair trial; the relationship of religion and government.

4. Examine the roles of civil rights advocates (e.g., A. Philip Randolph, Martin Luther King, Jr., Malcom X, Thurgood Marshall, James Farmer, Rosa Parks), including the significance of Martin Luther King, Jr.'s "Letter from Birmingham Jail" and "I Have a Dream" speech.

War Zones (2002)

I wrote this for my people.

We the types jumping out of street gutters
and man hole covers.
I ran with brothers that came straight from the sewers
the type to give Freddy Kruger a nightmare.
Young folks of color without a care in the world
who ain't afraid to die,
from the Southside to the east
we war with the beast.
Police send in their calvary new battalions
while I'm freestyling rounds from under a broken street light
from a sniper's distance
with pen point accuracy
to cause confusion on the premisses.
To make sure that we safely retreat
but some of us won't make it back to the street.
Prisoners of war
held in detention camps with names like
Elmwood,
San Quentin,
Soledad Maximum Security Prison.
I spit with conviction
until I get dizzy.
Stay camouflage by the foliage of the city
backtrack to the barracks
stay away from generic soldiers
turncoats,
possible informants
young folks hollowed out by
federal torments.
Reintroduced to the game
to prevent the gains
of the side they used to fight for.
If you didn't know by now this life is war.
Whether you believe it or not
we squeeze shots to ease tension on the block.
Avoid lockdown,
David versus Goliath.
We triumph with
justified violence.
Fling rocks blessed by the Most High
from sling shots
concealed in pockets of our baggy exterior.
With name brands like Akademiks
because the mission is truth.

Salute my folks with the words of peace
not knowing if our eyes will meet again.
Just knowing that we fought for what was right in the end,
the end,
the end
war zones,
war zones
that we're forced to call home.

My pants sag when I walk to show ain't nothing you can tell me.
Every social institution you created has failed me.
All you do is kill and jail me
to wipe out my chromosomes.
So every block
I walk
filled with cops
is a war zone,
a war zone.

Most likely seen running from cops in Reebok high tops
because they got
high ankle support.
Got to get free
alive you ain't taking me.
Ain't trying to see the inside of a court,
jury of my peers,
even if innocent
they'll make me serve 10 years.
There goes the prime of my life time,
so when we hear them sirens
iron is flying
under the night stars and sky line.
Ain't trying to see a cell with iron bars
repel down the sides of building walls
with a camouflage beanie around my noggin.
We move in secrecy like Bin Laden.
Communicate with young soldier
with chips in Motorolas
and Two-Way Nextell.
Who accustomed to having they flesh swelled
by them demons,
them devils with the letters PD on they lapel.
They get done up like Latrell Sprewell.
So cold,
because little Lakim got hit
with a Radio Raheem chokehold.
He 12 years old,
snot nosed
armed with a snow cone.

They said it was a handgun,
they chocked him until he coughed blood on his And 1's.
I'm told this is how they have fun,
and one comrade named his magnum
Adil,
the Arabic word for justice.
The enemy tries to crush us,
this oppression hugs us.
Don't question our actions,
only God can judge us.

Vocabulary Study Chart: "War Zones"

Word	Definition(s) and Synonym(s)	Copy the line or sentence from the text.	Your own example sentence
Calvary			
Battalions			
Premises			
Conviction			

Word	Definition(s) and Synonym(s)	Copy the line or sentence from the text.	Your own example sentence
Foliage			
Turncoats			
Chromosomes			

Black Boy Poems Research Learning Experience

In the chapter for the poem "War Zones" Tyson Amir equates the "fight" in our communities to the fight of Arjuna in the Bhagavad Gita. Learners will become familiar with the story and dilemma of Arjuna and use it to compare and contrast with the current context.

Who is Arjuna? What is his background, and where is he from?

In what text is the story of Arjuna told? How old is the story?

Summarize the backdrop of the conflict that Arjuna is faced with? What is his moral/ethical dilemma? How does he choose to deal with it before his advisor speaks to him?

Who does he meet, who attempts to counsel him? Who does his advisor reveal himself to be?

What advice does he receive? What is the justification for the actions he is supposed to take?

What were the fates of the main characters involved in the conflict?

The poem "War Zones" equates the neighborhoods/blocks that we walk to battlefields. The song is an extended metaphor describing the urban conditions that some communities live in as war zones. What lines in the poem describe aspects of these "war zones"?

In the poem who is the fight between and what is the goal of the parties fighting? Who in our current society represents the parties described in the poem? Explain why. Do you believe their fight is justified? Explain. Do you believe their fight will end? Explain.

"The Rose"

The Rose

Themes:

- Langston Hughes "Dream Deferred"

- Conscription (making learners familiar with the term and historically instances of conscription)

- Homophones (hands stay closed, schools close and homes foreclose, seems so close)

- Deconstructed literary devices (financial district/geographic jurisdiction and the jurist in my district…)

- thematic writing using the language of war. I do this a lot. War zones as well.
  - War is of attrition, fatigue and fatigues. (I also used this scheme of exhaustive war terminology to express the context of fighting and the cost of that fighting. It's a tiresome fight.

Prerequisites and Scaffolding:

There are a number of historical references towards the end of the poem. It's important for the learners to have some contextual understanding of what's being referenced to grasp its significance in those line of the poem.

- The Rose That Grew From Concrete by Tupac Shakur

- Angel Island

- Ellis Island

- Migration to reservations

- Bracero programs

- Sharecropping

Curriculum Implementation:

1. Initial Poem Reflection Learning Experience

2. Vocabulary Learning Experience

3. Second Poem Reflection Learning Experience

4. Unique Learning Experiences: The Rose

This chapter has two unique LEs.

The first of the two LEs asks the learners to determine where on the spectrum of the school-to-prison pipeline is their school. If learners are not familiar with the concept of the school to prison pipeline, then this LE will help give them some foundational understanding of what it is. It will also empower them to think critically about what resources are being provided to them.

The second LE give the learners an opportunity to reflect on their experience with school. The good, the bad and everything else. It also prompts them to think critically about how education is delivered, and what ideas they have about how the education process can be improved.

5. Deep Dive Poetry Analysis/Literary Device Learning Experience

6. Chapter Review Learning Experience

Expansion LEs:

Read the ACLU's full report on the school to prison pipeline and have the learners respond to it.

The Corridor film

Dave Mosenkis research

https://powerinterfaith.org/wp-content/uploads/2016/08/PA-Racial-School-Funding-Bias-July-2016-1-1.pdf

The Rose

Chronological and Spatial Thinking

Students compare the present with the past, evaluating the consequences of past events and decisions and determining the lessons that were learned.

Students analyze how change happens at different rates at different times; understand that some aspects can change while others remain the same; and understand that change is complicated and affects not only technology and politics but also values and beliefs.

Historical Research, Evidence, and Point of View

Students distinguish valid arguments from fallacious arguments in historical interpretations.

Students identify bias and prejudice in historical interpretations.

Students evaluate major debates among historians concerning alternative interpretations of the past, including an analysis of authors' use of evidence and the distinctions between sound generalizations and misleading oversimplifications.

Students construct and test hypotheses; collect, evaluate, and employ information from multiple primary and secondary sources; and apply it in oral and written presentations.

Historical Interpretation

Students show the connections, causal and otherwise, between particular historical events and larger social, economic, and political trends and developments.

Students recognize the complexity of historical causes and effects, including the limitations on determining cause and effect.

Students interpret past events and issues within the context in which an event unfolded rather than solely in terms of present-day norms and values.

Students understand the meaning, implication, and impact of historical events and recognize that events could have taken other directions.

Standards and learning objectives:

5. Trace the development of the American education system from its earliest roots, including the roles of religious and private schools and Horace Mann's campaign for free public education and its assimilating role in American culture.

2. Study the roles of people in each society, including class structures, family life, war fare, religious beliefs and practices, and slavery.

6. Analyze the persistence of poverty and how different analyses of this issue influence welfare reform, health insurance reform, and other social policies.

7. Explain how the federal, state, and local governments have responded to demographic and social changes such as population shifts to the suburbs, racial concentrations in the cities, Frostbelt-to-Sunbelt migration, international migration, decline of family farms, increases in out-of-wedlock births, and drug abuse.

The Rose (2015)

I'll attempt to collect my thoughts to show you all what I've been thinking through.

It's just a humble depiction of the conditions
some of these men and women I know on the brink have been through.

Word to the wise: don't hold your breath waiting for this society to save you
because if you do, then you'll soon be blinking blue.

In the eyes of many, we belong to
a disease infested, decrepit stinking few.

Stranded in gentrified neighborhoods where it's hard to survive
levees breaking got us sinking too.
Call it (Katrina Redux)

Meanwhile, constantly seeping through cracks
are noxious toxic chemicals.
Asthma and cancer are perennial visitors
to where we sleeping through.

Now can y'all see me move?
See what I speak take you in and out of these streets
quicker than them policemen do.
That last line wasn't a swipe at the boys in blue.
what I'm speaking is deeper than that.
this is designed to define everything outside in our environment set to poison me and you.

I once heard from one of our elders by the name of Langston Hughes

The question of the deferred dream.

And it's sad that when we even have to consider such an absurd thing.

That for some boys and girls
that word means
something less tangible.

That it's harder for them to grab a handful,

so their hands stay closed.

Just as schools close and homes foreclose,
yet it still seems so close.

Like when you standing on the corner of Jones and Post
where you can see the wealth of Union Square vivid and up close,
but it's

oh

so

far.

That financial district might as well be another geographic jurisdiction.

And the jurist in my district
don't understand that the blocks we're from force conscription.

Men and women are drafted from the womb
to be at war with the system.

There are very few ways to make it out,
and everyday it gets harder to pick them.

And this war is of attrition.
The fatigue bleeds deep into our bones.
The fatigues we wear look like
white tees, jeans, air ones, fitted cap over the dome.

But we're soldiers of misfortune
because we don't even know what we're fighting for.

Is it for the hood, or for the block?
Is it for the good, or for the guap?
Is it for the dead homie who just waiting for the next dead homie to drop?

Y'all we so confused,
we so traumatized and so abused.

But still in this midst of all this, did y'all hear what Pac said,

Did you hear about the rose that grew?

From a crack in the concrete.
Yeah, we got crack up and down our concrete
but even through that trap
the rose grew.
And that rose is you.

Through underfunded schools,
the war on poverty,
the war on drugs,
the war on terror
the war on our young,
prison industrial complex,

bracero programs,
united farm workers,
civil rights,
jim crow,
forced migration to reservations,
Ellis and Angel island,
sharecropping and slavery.
We've survived it all.

We're made strong by the legacy of those that came before us,
now we triumphantly march into the greatness of our moment.

But don't be mistaken,
see the matrix is quick to shape-shift.
It'll try to take that faith you have in yourself
and make you an atheist.

It'll try to get you
to forget
what this date is.
But we will never forget,
that on the 18th day of June
in the year two thousand and fifteen,
a rose grew.

In the face of all things attempting to stifle it,
it still bloomed.

And it's bloom yields all these incredible hues.

Strengthened by the struggle
found in our soil and our roots.

It doesn't matter what they do
everyday this is what we need from you.

Stand tall,
greet the sun,
shine bright and bold
and give your beautiful brilliance to us all.

That's what a rose would do,
and that rose is you.

Vocabulary Study Chart: "The Rose"

Word	Definition(s) and Synonym(s)	Copy the line or sentence from the poem/reflection	Your own example sentence
Decrepit			
Gentrified			
Redux			
Noxious			

Word	Definition(s) and Synonym(s)	Copy the line or sentence from the poem/reflection	Your own example sentence
Perennial			
Tangible			
Jurisdiction			
Attrition			

Word	Definition(s) and Synonym(s)	Copy the line or sentence from the poem/reflection	Your own example sentence
Atheist			
Stifle			

Black Boy Poems Research Learning Experience

Personal Connection

How would you describe your experience with school?

How much have you learned about yourself and the history of your people in your education career? If you feel you haven't learned much, then why do think that is happening in your school experience?

How much have you learned in your educational experience about the issues we are facing in our society and how you can influence them?

How much have you learned about the conditions in your community and how you can influence them?

Quote Responses

In the text Tyson Amir wrote, "Our path to freedom and liberation is only possible through knowledge and a strict revolutionary application of what we will learn." What do you believe Tyson is attempting to say in this section?

"If we only depend on our school experience to provide us with a foundation for our futures, then we are doomed to the same tragic existence, if not worse, that black folks have experienced in America." What does this quote mean to you in light of your school experience?

Read and respond to the quote by George Jackson in the first paragraph on page 153. What is the meaning of what he said? How does your personal school experience reflect this statement?

Critical reflection and response

List some of the positives and negatives you feel exist in the public school system today? What changes do you think should take place in schools to allow for a more empowering education experience?

If the people responsible for "educating" you are not doing that job, then whose responsibility is it? What do you feel should be taught in schools to empower learners? In what ways would you change the curriculum and school environment? Be as creative as possible.

Black Boy Poems Research Learning Experience

Prior Knowledge:

What is the school to prison pipeline?

How did the school to prison pipeline develop? Who profits from the school to prison pipeline? Who are the people most impacted by the school to prison pipeline?

Analyze and Respond:

"A 2003 report published by the Bureau of Justice & Statistics titled 'Education and Correctional Populations' stated that 68 percent of the state prison population then had not received a high-school diploma."

"The correlation between lack of education and jail and prison is thoroughly documented by more agencies than just the BJS. One of the more popular social/political buzzwords of the day is the school-to-prison pipeline. The American Civil Liberties Union states, "The 'school-to-prison pipeline' refers to the policies and practices that push our nation's schoolchildren, especially our most at-risk children, out of classrooms and into the juvenile and criminal justice systems. This pipeline reflects the prioritization of incarceration over education." "

"How do we arrive at the school to prison pipeline? The ACLU highlights multiple points; we'll look at a few. "For most students, the pipeline begins with inadequate resources in public schools. Overcrowded classrooms, a lack of qualified teachers, and insufficient funding for "extras" such as counselors, special education services, and even textbooks, lock students into second-rate educational environments. This failure to meet educational needs increases disengagement and dropouts, increasing the risk of later court involvement. Even worse, schools may actually encourage dropouts in response to pressures from test-based accountability regimes such as the No Child Left Behind Act, which create incentives to push out low-performing students to boost overall test scores."

Is your school on the spectrum of the school to prison pipeline?

One common aspect of schools on the spectrum of the school to prison pipeline is zero tolerance policies. Does your school have zero tolerance policies? If so, what students are impacted the most by zero tolerance policies?

Another common element in the school to prison pipeline are schools with inadequate resources for educating students? Does your school have "adequate" resources for students' education? Does your school district have "adequate" resources for the students in the district? How much funding is allocated for student resources?

Another aspect of the school to prison pipeline is the increased use of police or school officers on school grounds. Does your school have police/security officers? If so, how many? In your opinion, does the presence of school/police officers in your learning space make the environment feel more like an incarceration facility or a school? Explain.

What are the graduation rates for students in your school and district? Analyze those statistics along lines of ethnicity and gender.

Based on your research do you believe your school is participating in funneling students to the jail/prison side of the school to prison pipeline? Explain. What do you believe should be done to dismantle the school to prison pipeline? Explain.

Black Boy Poems Curriculum

"The Dirge"

The Dirge

Themes:

- Death is an important theme in this piece. I believe this provides an opportunity for exploring how different peoples throughout time and space have dealt with the reality of death in their particular cultures.

- The Dirge is a representation of how cultural artifacts are present in many funerary traditions. Poetry and writings about death. To commemorate/remember those who have passed.

- Other dirge examples in music and culture.

Prerequisites and Scaffolding:

Similar to other pieces in this collection, I make a number of historical references that the learners should have some context for.

- Nina, Pinta and Santa Maria

- 1619 when the first 19 of us got off

- Holocaust

- Layman's terms

- Repetition (literary device)

Curriculum Implementation:

1. Initial Poem Reflection Learning Experience

2. Vocabulary Learning Experience

3. Second Poem Reflection Learning Experience

4. Unique Learning Experiences: The Dirge

This chapter has two unique LEs.

The first of the two LEs for this chapter has the learners researching homicide victimization rates from three different sources, the BJS, Violence Policy Center and the United Nations. The primary goal is for learners to begin to see the disparate life chances for peoples depending on where they are, who they are and how much money they have.

The second LE brings the learners in contact with the constitution's 15th amendment and 18th president of the United States, Ulysseys S Grant. In 1876 while still presdient, Ulysseys S Grant's commented on the 15th amendment stating, "it had done the Negro no good and had been a hindrance to the South and by no means a political advantage to the North." The LE asks the learners to consider the historic and contemporary reality of voter disenfranchisement.

5. Deep Dive Poetry Analysis/Literary Device Learning Experience

6. Chapter Review Learning Experience

Expansion LEs:

I talk about Tamir Rice's case. Research the actual language in Timothy Loehmann's <u>file</u> from Independence, Ohio. (Pgs. 59-60 of TL's file)

Research Gwendolyn Brooks' piece We Real Cool

Creating opportunities for the learners to become more familiar with all the family's present in the gathering I attended and wrote "The Dirge" for.

The Dirge

Chronological and Spatial Thinking

Students compare the present with the past, evaluating the consequences of past events and decisions and determining the lessons that were learned.

Students analyze how change happens at different rates at different times; understand that some aspects can change while others remain the same; and understand that change is complicated and affects not only technology and politics but also values and beliefs.

Students relate current events to the physical and human characteristics of places and regions.

Historical Research, Evidence, and Point of View

Students distinguish valid arguments from fallacious arguments in historical interpretations.

Students identify bias and prejudice in historical interpretations.

Students evaluate major debates among historians concerning alternative interpretations of the past, including an analysis of authors' use of evidence and the distinctions between sound generalizations and misleading oversimplifications.

Students construct and test hypotheses; collect, evaluate, and employ information from multiple primary and secondary sources; and apply it in oral and written presentations.

Historical Interpretation

Students show the connections, causal and otherwise, between particular historical events and larger social, economic, and political trends and developments.

Students recognize the complexity of historical causes and effects, including the limitations on determining cause and effect.

Students interpret past events and issues within the context in which an event unfolded rather than solely in terms of present-day norms and values.

Students understand the meaning, implication, and impact of historical events and recognize that events could have taken other directions.

Standards and Learning objectives

4. Discuss Abraham Lincoln's presidency and his significant writings and speeches and their relationship to the Declaration of Independence, such as his "House Divided" speech (1858), Gettysburg Address (1863), Emancipation Proclamation (1863), and inaugural addresses (1861 and 1865).

5. Study the views and lives of leaders (e.g., Ulysses S. Grant, Jefferson Davis, Robert E. Lee) and soldiers on both sides of the war, including those of black soldiers and regiments.

Students analyze the character and lasting consequences of Reconstruction.

The Dirge (2014)

You hear the dirge of the funeral march
as the band plays on.
And instantly my heart recognizes it as the same song,
played since the days of slave songs,
which means I'm going to stand here until the flame is gone
or the pain is gone
because I don't know how many more names like Oscar and Trayvon
we'll have to play it for.

The populous doesn't watch out for us
nor acknowledge us.
They simply dismiss our cries for help as obnoxious
until they're presented to them in a form worthy of being nominated for an oscar
by some Academy for the best actor and score.
But sadly
this is the madness that maddens me
and the savagery that surrounds me
in the streets that we inhabit be
growing exponentially evermore.

Four score and some odd years ago,
man, I can't even keep score.
And if there is a scoreboard of how many of our loved ones
have become extinct and are now no more,
just that simple thought of that makes me want to cry
until my tear ducts are sore.
Or scream until my voice and vocal chords become hoarse,
the only lawful alternative is to
unleash this force through verse.
Capable of leaving pages and earth scorched
because the truth hurts,
that to them we are nothing more.

How many more Amadou Diallos and Abner Louimas?
But it's been foretold
since the days of The Nina, Pinta and Santa Maria,
or 1619 when the first 19 of us got off,
or should I say got lost.
Involuntarily drafted into this American Holocaust.
You ask about the cost.
It can't be computed by some consumer price index.
We go from slavery to Jim Crow
to prison industrial complex
punctuated by a death sentence.
Sentenced to reside in a land
where they rally behind stand your ground

which in layman's terms we know means another nigger down.
Translated to black speak
we know it means it's open season on us now.

Can y'all feel that adrenaline rush now?

But I need y'all to hush now

Listening carefully
because the world is changing right now.
While we are busy entertaining,
skinny jeans sagging on corners hanging,
Molly popping and bo' sipping
weed smoking and banging;

they have crosshairs trained
on an entire generation.

They have prisons cells and guns aimed
at an entire generation.

Deemed expendable is
an entire generation.

The government does not care about
an entire generation.

We are the only ones who care about
an entire generation.

Therefore, we are the only ones who can save
an entire generation.

Vocabulary Study Chart: "The Dirge"

Word	Definition(s) and Synonym(s)	Copy the line or sentence from the text.	Your own example sentence
Dirge			
Exponentially			
Hoarse			
Layman/layperson			

Word	Definition(s) and Synonym(s)	Copy the line or sentence from the text.	Your own example sentence
Expendable			
Morbid			

Black Boy Poems Research Learning Experience

Read from 173-174 Beginning with the last paragraph on pg. 173

To put reduced life chances into context…

Finish with the last paragraph on pg. 174

I don't think you fully comprehend…

Personal connection

How much of this information were you aware of? What are your thoughts and feelings about these statistical findings? Explain.

Questions:

What do these numbers tell you about the life chances of black people in the United States?

Compare and contrast these numbers with the newest data by the VPC (Violence Policy Center). Make your analysis include gender and compare the black rate to the national rates of all groups including gender. http://www.vpc.org/studies/blackhomicide18.pdf

List your findings here:

Why do you feel these trends are so consistent year after year in the United States? Explain

Analyze the Victim/Offender Relationship, Circumstance data and info from your home state. What are the root causes to the majority of these homicides? What's the data for your home state?

Critical Analysis

The black homicide rate is largely influenced by the social/political/economic conditions of our society. If the conditions that create those circumstances change, then the instances of black homicide rates would change as well. However, we as a society are experiencing another very tragic phenomenon, the increase of instances of mass shootings. Analyze the data in these articles

https://www.theguardian.com/us-news/ng-interactive/2017/oct/02/america-mass-shootings-gun-violence

https://www.nytimes.com/2017/11/07/world/americas/mass-shootings-us-international.html?module=inline

According to the data, how often is there a mass shooting?

How many guns are in the United States?

What are the main commonalities between the perpetuators of these heinous acts?

What are the current politicians and authority figures doing about this issue? How would you change this current situation in our society? Explain. What steps do you and your fellow learners plan to take to do something about this issue. Explain.

Black Boy Poems Research Learning Experience

In 1876 President Ulysses S. Grant voiced to his cabinet his belief that the 15th Amendment to the constitution was a mistake, saying, "it had done the Negro no good and had been a hinderance to the South and by no means a political advantage to the North."

What is the significance of the 15th Amendment?

When and why was it added to the constitution?

How do you feel about President Grant's comments on black folks and the 15th amendment? Explain your answer.

Critical Thinking and Analysis

Voter disenfranchisement has played a major role in our past elections. Voter disenfranchisement still plays a role in our contemporary elections. In this section you'll begin to analyze some of the history and present reality of voter disenfranchisement.

What groups have historically been targeted the most by voter disenfranchisement? List examples of ways that these communities have been systemically disenfranchised.

What communities present in our society today are experiencing voter disenfranchisement? List examples of how these communities are currently being disenfranchised.

In what ways do you see connections between President Ulysses S. Grant's comments in 1876 and the reality of present day voter disenfranchisement experienced by various communities?

What solutions would you attempt to implement to solve the issue of voter disenfranchisement? Explain.

Black Boy Poems Curriculum

"Letter to Johnetta"

Letter to Johnetta

Themes:

- Black Feminism

- White Feminism

- Feminism

- Patriarchy

- Male Privilege

- Societal exploitation of women. Taking a real look at how our society has disadvantaged women, especially black women and other women of color.

Prerequisites and Scaffolding:

- Exploring the ideas and history of black feminism. It is very different from what feminism has looked like in the possession of white women.

- The depth of the mistreatment of black women in this society.

- <u>Black Women in the United States</u>.

Curriculum Implementation:

1. Initial Poem Reflection Learning Experience

2. Vocabulary Learning Experience

3. Second Poem Reflection Learning Experience

4. Unique Learning Experiences: Letter to Johnetta

This chapter has two unique LEs and an additional LE that could be used as a way to cover some of the prerequisites and scaffolding ideas.

The first LE in this section has the learners participating in a research project. Hip Hop can be a very powerful instrument for change. In order to live up to its fullest potential it can't be used as a weapon that brings harm to populations that will be necessary in helping to create that change. In this light the learners will analyze Hip Hop and its depiction of Black women and women in general. In addition to its depiction of women, they will also analyze Hip Hop for its usage of images and terminology that disrespects the LGBTQ community.

Our second LE has the learners researching the traditions of revolutionary women from different historical and cultural backgrounds. The LE can be done individually or in a group.

5. Deep Dive Poetry Analysis/Literary Device Learning Experience

6. Chapter Review Learning Experience

Expansion LEs:

Analysis of bell hooks' quote on patriarchy from The will to Change

Audre Lorde's statement in the text.

Dr. Cornel West's quote

Sarah Bartman

Letter to Johnetta

Chronological and Spatial Thinking

Students compare the present with the past, evaluating the consequences of past events and decisions and determining the lessons that were learned.

Students analyze how change happens at different rates at different times; understand that some aspects can change while others remain the same; and understand that change is complicated and affects not only technology and politics but also values and beliefs.

Historical Research, Evidence, and Point of View

Students distinguish valid arguments from fallacious arguments in historical interpretations.

Students identify bias and prejudice in historical interpretations.

Students evaluate major debates among historians concerning alternative interpretations of the past, including an analysis of authors' use of evidence and the distinctions between sound generalizations and misleading oversimplifications.

Students construct and test hypotheses; collect, evaluate, and employ information from multiple primary and secondary sources; and apply it in oral and written presentations.

Historical Interpretation

Students show the connections, causal and otherwise, between particular historical events and larger social, economic, and political trends and developments.

Students recognize the complexity of historical causes and effects, including the limitations on determining cause and effect.

Students interpret past events and issues within the context in which an event unfolded rather than solely in terms of present-day norms and values.

Students understand the meaning, implication, and impact of historical events and recognize that events could have taken other directions.

Standards and Learning objectives

Evaluate the major debates that occurred during the development of the Constitution and their ultimate resolutions in such areas as shared power among institutions, divided state-federal power, slavery, the rights of individuals and states (later addressed by the addition of the Bill of Rights), and the status of American Indian nations under the commerce clause.

1. Analyze the principles and concepts codified in state constitutions between 1777 and 1781 that created the context out of which American political institutions and ideas developed.

7. Analyze the women's rights movement from the era of Elizabeth Stanton and Susan Anthony and the passage of the Nineteenth Amendment to the movement launched in the 1960s, including differing perspectives on the roles of women.

3. Describe the changing roles of women in society as reflected in the entry of more women into the labor force and the changing family structure.

Letter to Johnetta (2015)

She's that fast talking,
lip popping,
teeth sucking,
often annoyed
quick to start something
with anybody over nothing
allowing everybody to push her imaginary button.
Forever beefing with her dude
and quick to cut him,
black girl.

Johnetta I see you.
I mean like for real for real I see you.
And I wish I had some magic power
or some latent mutant ability
that could allow you to see you for you.
Not what America tells you is you
not what these dudes in these raps songs say about you
or what the streets say you need to be,
but who you are for you.

The story goes:
Your pops probably wasn't around.
You and your moms might or might not be on good terms,
probably been to jail a few times.
Life took a couple u-turns.
That's probably how we met,
I was teaching up at the county and there you were.

It was my job was to teach you some math
or some new words.
Open up your mind to a new world
but in the process noticing how lost you were.
I asked you about your family
and you told me about your new girl.
What's your baby girl like?
"Ah, she's smart, she cute
but she hates it when I'm gone."
Where her daddy at?
"Oh, he locked up
he ain't gonna be coming home."

How you deal with that?
"Shoot, I on't even know."

What you gonna do when you get out?
"Uh, I ain't gonna do that much boosting anymore."

Or, *"I ain't gonna be getting high,*
I'm gonna get my babies this time.
Go back to school get me a GED
get me a cool 9 to 5."

But so often when they back to the streets
them dreams get cast off.
She go back to selling that kat off,
or getting them packs off.
Dreams of getting them stacks and them racks tall,
not knowing how we so thoroughly blackballed.

And this ain't no judgment
because it ain't our fault.
The government has historically made us into outlaws.

See, in slavery days, the slave master would make us watch
as he forcefully deflowered y'all.
Then crept to your quarters at night making them house calls.
And sadly, your king, meaning me
was without claws,
because without cause
he could hang me by my neck
from a tree with a string
until my heart paused.

Pause!

The system made it so we failed y'all,
and the strong women you are
you showed your resolve and evolved.
You had babies to raise.
Meals to cook and homes to make
in hopes that your babies wouldn't break
in the face of this American hate
that attempted to emasculate your man
and put us at odds in the first place.

Since then we trying to get our rhythm back.
America hating on everything that means living black.
Then we end up hating everything inside of us
that means the same thing in fact.

See, Johnetta I know all that,
but what I want now is our men and our women back.
The devil been feeding us lies

all that bitches and hoes,
bad bitch
trap queen
thug misses.
That ain't you,
that ain't us.
We are the inheritors of culture filled with riches.
They say the greatest of tricks ever performed is by the devil
making us doubt his existence.
And what I see happening to my brothers and sisters clearly
bares the mark of his imprint.
This letter is penned with hopes that you'll remember your beginnings.
Before this cloud of white hate descended
and sent us down a path or self hate and resentment.
This letter was penned in hopes that you'll remember your beginnings.
Please remember your beginnings, my beautiful brothers and sisters.
Please remember our beginnings.

Vocabulary Study Chart: "Letter to Johnetta"

Word	Definition(s) and Synonym(s)	Copy the line or sentence from the text.	Your own example sentence
Latent			
Blackballed			
Resolve			
Approximation			

Word	Definition(s) and Synonym(s)	Copy the line or sentence from the text.	Your own example sentence
Patriarchal			
Feminism			
Sexism			
Appropriation			

**Black Boy Poems** Research Learning Experience

Hip Hop and its depiction of Women and the LGBTQI community

Hip Hop can contribute in a significant way to movements focused on freedom, liberation, education and empowerment. However, one of the central contradictions with Hip Hop and its revolutionary potential is its use of derogatory/demeaning and antagonistic images of women and the LGBTQI community. Both groups will need to play important roles in any movement for freedom and liberation. This analysis is not done to bash Hip Hop. Hip Hop is a byproduct of Western hyper masculine patriarchal culture. This is why you can find similar negative depictions of women and the LGBTQI community in other industries and genres of media. We are focusing on Hip Hop because it has the greatest revolutionary potential and is the most popular form of artistic expression in the world today, especially among youth.

Pick at least 3 of the the most popular songs and videos from male and female artists from these eras of Hip Hop: 85-89, 90-94, 95-99, 2000-2004, 2005-2009, 2010-2014 and 2015 to the present. In your analysis of the songs and videos you'll examine:

How are women portrayed in the song?

How are men portrayed in the song?

Is there any language or references in the song/video that impugn members of the LGBTQI community?

What's the overall tone of the song towards women? Explain your rationale.

189

Do you believe the song/video presents a positive or negative image of women? How relevant was the depiction of women to the overall focus of the song? Explain.

Extended analysis:

Compare your results with other popular genres of music because Hip Hop is not an anomaly when it comes to representation issues. (Feel free to explore other genres that are more reflective of the musical tastes of your learners)

Rock
Country
Punk
R&B
Pop
Salsa
Other forms of cultural music

Why do you believe these images are some prevalent in the lyrics and visual depictions in Hip Hop and other genres of music? Do you feel these images are sound representations of girls and women?

Do you believe it is possible to use a tool (Hip Hop) for positive/liberation purposes when a core aspect of how it's shared with the people is to demean peoples who are necessary for that positive/liberation cause? Explain your answer.

Black Boy Poems Research Learning Experience

Prior Knowledge Connections:

What women are you aware of who participated in revolutionary movements? What were you taught about these figures?

In this LE you will select two names from the list of Revolutionary Women and answer the following questions.

Research questions:

Where is your revolutionary woman from?

What era did she live in?

What was her path to becoming a political/revolutionary figure? What major social/political context was she fighting against? What reasons did she have for getting involved in that struggle?

What strategies did she use for contributing to the struggle she was involved in?

How successful was she in her efforts?

Are there any male contemporaries that she had who receive more attention for their work? Are there any male contemporaries who receive credit for the work your revolutionary woman was responsible for?

How has she been remembered by history? What type of legacy did she establish?

Why do you feel the story and legacy of your research subject isn't as widely known as it should be? Explain.

Harriet Tubman (USA)

Queen Nzinga (Angola)

Ida B. Wells (USA)

Fannie Lou Hamer (USA)

Elaine Brown (USA)

Yuri Kochiyama (USA)

Yuma Zeinab (Eritrea)

Grace Lee Bogs (USA)

Troung Sisters (Viet-Nam)

Winnie Mandela (South Africa)

Buffalo Calf Road Woman (Northern Chyenne)

Dolores Huerta (Chicana)

Celia Sanchez (Cuba)

Vilma Espin (Cuba)

Juana Azurduy (Bolivian)

Mirabal Sisters (Dominican Republic)

Lakshmi Sahgal (India)

Berta Caseres (Honduran)

Qiu Jin (China)

Queen Nanny (Jamaica)

Blanca Canales (Puerto Rico)

Black Boy Poems Research Learning Experience

This LE provides learners with an opportunity to begin developing an in depth analysis of the position of women in our society today. Specifically the position of women of color, even more specifically the position of black women.

Defining Terms:
Create definitions of these terms based on your understanding of what they mean. Compare and contrast your definitions with dictionary/ institutional definitions of these same terms.

Sexism -

Patriarchy -

Black Feminism -

Feminism -

White Feminism -

Gender Inequality -

Without doing any research, estimate the amount of money you think these groups earn on average for every **dollar** a white man earns in the USA. Answer in cents. For example 0.75 cents or 0.60 cents.

Latino Man		White Woman	
Black Man		Latina Woman	
Asian Man		Black Woman	
Native/Indigenous Man		Asian Woman	
		Native/Indigenous Woman	

Use these resources below to see the dollar comparisons for these groups of people.

Resource for women

Resource for men and women
Another resource

https://www.businessinsider.com/gender-wage-pay-gap-charts-2017-3#women-with-children-are-penalized-while-men-with-children-are-rewarded-4

What are the average amounts that these groups earn in comparison with white male earnings?

Latino Man		White Woman	
Black Man		Latina Woman	
Asian Man		Black Woman	
Native/Indigenous Man		Asian Woman	
		Native/Indigenous Woman	

Wealth inequality is just one way that we are able to see how our patriarchal society unfairly discriminates against women. That discrimination and oppression is not relegated to that one area. It manifests in other areas as well. Depending on which group of women we are looking at the restrictions placed on their lived experience could be even more harsh.

Analysis and response

https://www.americanprogress.org/issues/women/news/
2013/09/25/75076/explore-the-data-the-state-of-women-in-america/

https://www.americanprogress.org/issues/race/reports/
2012/07/17/11923/the-state-of-women-of-color-in-the-united-states/

https://www.npr.org/assets/news/2017/12/discriminationpoll-women.pdf

Black Women in the United States Report analysis

Black Boy Poems Curriculum

"Material of Martyrs"

Material of Martyrs

Themes:

- Double entendre

- Literal and figurative language

- schematic/thematic writing which includes references to mercantilism, industrialism, mechanical production and the textile industry. Capitalism.

- Alliteration

Prerequisites and Scaffolding:

- The real "cost" of capitalism (the land stolen from indigenous peoples, the lives lost, the theft, exploitation of millions of men, women and children from the african continent for centuries.)

- European countries and eventually the United States became wealthy and powerful by engaging in one of the most barbaric epochs in the history of our species. Then attempted to sanitize it and justify it by calling it entrepreneurism, free market capitalism and a number of other euphemisms that cloak the brutality of stealing, murdering and enslaving for power and profit.

- Historical figures:
    - Medgar Evers
    - Trayvon Martin
    - Sandra Bland

- The history of lynching in this country. EJI and museum dedicated to lynching. I'm clad in that plaid pattern rope makes on flesh when tied around necks as nooses.

- Burning crosses, ballot boxes brutality making us into burnt offerings at the altar.

- Burnt offering (sacrifice for the material wealth, power and mental health of this land/people)

Curriculum Implementation:

1. Initial Poem Reflection Learning Experience

2. Vocabulary Learning Experience

3. Second Poem Reflection Learning Experience

4. Unique Learning Experiences: Material of Martyrs

This chapter has one unique LE.

Learners will get the opportunity to analyze aspects of the contemporary global capitalistic system. The will study certain terminology and research a chain of production from natural resource to good/service on the market. They will then examine how much exploited/stolen labor is necessary for them to live the life they are accustomed to.

5. Deep Dive Poetry Analysis/Literary Device Learning Experience

6. Chapter Review Learning Experience

Expansion LEs:

Wealth disparities in the USA and world. Analysis of wealthiest people in comparison with wealth for the rest of the people on the planet.

EJI history of lynching

The Half Has Never Been Told

Material of Martyrs

Chronological and Spatial Thinking

Students compare the present with the past, evaluating the consequences of past events and decisions and determining the lessons that were learned.

Students analyze how change happens at different rates at different times; understand that some aspects can change while others remain the same; and understand that change is complicated and affects not only technology and politics but also values and beliefs.

Students use a variety of maps and documents to interpret human movement, including major patterns of domestic and international migration, changing environmental preferences and settlement patterns, the frictions that develop between population groups, and the diffusion of ideas, technological innovations, and goods.

Students relate current events to the physical and human characteristics of places and regions.

Historical Research, Evidence, and Point of View

Students distinguish valid arguments from fallacious arguments in historical interpretations.

Students identify bias and prejudice in historical interpretations.

Students evaluate major debates among historians concerning alternative interpretations of the past, including an analysis of authors' use of evidence and the distinctions between sound generalizations and misleading oversimplifications.

Students construct and test hypotheses; collect, evaluate, and employ information from multiple primary and secondary sources; and apply it in oral and written presentations.

Historical Interpretation

Students show the connections, causal and otherwise, between particular historical events and larger social, economic, and political trends and developments.

Students recognize the complexity of historical causes and effects, including the limitations on determining cause and effect.

Students interpret past events and issues within the context in which an event unfolded rather than solely in terms of present-day norms and values.

Students understand the meaning, implication, and impact of historical events and recognize that events could have taken other directions.

Students analyze human modifications of landscapes and examine the resulting environmental policy issues.

Students conduct cost-benefit analyses and apply basic economic indicators to analyze the aggregate economic behavior of the U.S. economy.

Standards and Learning objectives

3. Examine the origins of modern capitalism; the influence of mercantilism and cottage industry; the elements and importance of a market economy in seventeenth-century Europe; the changing international trading and marketing patterns, including their locations on a world map; and the influence of explorers and map makers.

3. Analyze the rise of capitalism and the economic problems and conflicts that accompanied it (e.g., Jackson's opposition to the National Bank; early decisions of the U.S. Supreme Court that reinforced the sanctity of contracts and a capitalist economic system of law).

Discuss the influence of industrialization and technological developments on the region, including human modification of the landscape and how physical geography shaped human actions (e.g., growth of cities, deforestation, farming, mineral extraction).

1. Describe the development of the agrarian economy in the South, identify the locations of the cotton-producing states, and discuss the significance of cotton and the cotton gin.

2. Trace the origins and development of slavery; its effects on black Americans and on the region's political, social, religious, economic, and cultural development; and identify the strategies that were tried to both overturn and preserve it (e.g., through the writings and historical documents on Nat Turner, Denmark Vesey).

3. Examine the characteristics of white Southern society and how the physical environment influenced events and conditions prior to the Civil War.

4. Compare the lives of and opportunities for free blacks in the North with those of free blacks in the South.

12.1 Students understand common economic terms and concepts and economic reasoning.

1. Examine the causal relationship between scarcity and the need for choices.

2. Explain opportunity cost and marginal benefit and marginal cost.

4. Evaluate the role of private property as an incentive in conserving and improving scarce resources, including renewable and nonrenewable natural resources.

1. Understand the relationship of the concept of incentives to the law of supply and the relationship of the concept of incentives and substitutes to the law of demand.

2. Discuss the effects of changes in supply and/or demand on the relative scarcity, price, and quantity of particular products.

3. Explain the roles of property rights, competition, and profit in a market economy.

Material of Martyrs (2015)

I am made from the material of martyrs.
Hewn in the hollows of vessels whose hulls housed
the most horrific horrors history has known.

Fashioned in a furnace
fueled by the fires of hatred and fear.

I emerge mangled and misshapen.
The merciless hands of manufacturers
attempt to molest my essence,
maneuvering my body in multiple directions.

Am I not man and brother?
Am I not flesh and bone?

Their eye is incapable of envisioning that reality,
my truth is engulfed.
Superimposed are their mental projections,
byproducts of their fantasy and fancy.

They cannot see
that I too
am blessed By the One.
Adorned in a bold, brilliant
and beautiful brocaded dark cloth.
Eerily iridescent
incandescent
and majestic.

Their eyes marvel,
and then their envy intervenes.
Their hearts conspire jealousy.
Their souls grows deficient and desperate.

Their desire is to own the economy of me.
Incarcerate those of this ilk.
Appropriate our creations
for the expressed purposes
of commodity and control.

And they believe their victory is nigh.

But what they don't know is
intricately woven into the fabrics of our robes
are rebellion and resistance.

Yeah, these wears are wrought with revolution.

Regalia ripe with the royal hues of our royal ancestry.

Garments replete with struggle and survival.
Bespoke apparel
customized by
the knowledge and wisdom
amplified by
shotgun shells flying through those barrels in the Audubon.

No brand names,
just black names
in each strand of cotton,
linen,
silk,
polyester
and rayon
I have on.

I wear Addie Mae Collins,
Denise McNair,
Carole Robertson,
Cynthia Wesley,
Medgar Evers
and Trayvon.

I'm covered in some Martin King,
Fred Hampton,
Fred Gray
Emmett Till,
Sandra Bland.

I'm clad in that plaid pattern
rope make on flesh
when tied around necks
as nooses.

This is not some fashion week exclusive.

This is bruises and blood,
bullets and billy clubs,
burning crosses,
ballot boxes,
brutality making us into
burnt offerings at the altar.

If you look here, my man, you'll see
this ain't swag.

This is sophistication
stitched through generations.
It's deep in them lines and them seams.
And my kind knows the reality
of what every thread means.

You can't buy that.
You can't try that.
It's not off the rack
or couture.
This that authentic black culture.

And I've found this cut and fit
is tailored to my size.
Ain't no other suit for me to try,
nor would I want to try,
and this is why I make this look so good,
because I wear this with pride.

Vocabulary Study Chart: "Material of Martyrs"

Word	Definition(s) and Synonym(s)	Copy the line or sentence from the text.	Your own example sentence
Hewn			
Hulls			
Adorned			
Iridescent			

Word	Definition(s) and Synonym(s)	Copy the line or sentence from the text.	Your own example sentence
Incandescent			
Nigh			
Wrought			
Replete			

Word	Definition(s) and Synonym(s)	Copy the line or sentence from the poem/reflection	Your own example sentence
Clad			
Burnt Offering			

Black Boy Poems Research Learning Experience

In the poem "Material of Martyrs" Tyson Amir attempts to bring attention to the historical barbarity of Capitalism by bringing attention to the ways that it has prioritized profits over people. He chose to begin his poem with the theft and trafficking of black bodies from the African continent. He then connects that to the institution of forced servitude for profit. One of the primary uses of that stolen labor was providing "cheap" cash crops for the industrial demand for textiles. This brings us to the concept of material. The title can be understood as a double entendre because it speaks to the idea of the clothing material that was produced and the genetic material that produced a people.

Basic principles of capitalism. Give a brief definition of each.

Profit

Market

Invisible Hand

Demand

Supply

Labor

Capital

Means of production

Industry

Property

Exploitation

Goods and services

Resources

Cash Crop

Research a chain of production

Pick a manufactured product from the list below and research its chain of production. What materials are needed to make it? Where do the materials come from? Where is the product manufactured? Who is it made by? How are those laborers treated? How much do the laborers get paid for their work? How much does the product cost to be made? What is the sale price of the product in the market?

- iPhone or other "smart phone", tablet or video game system
- Jordans or other popular brand shoe
- Designer Jeans or some other designer clothing item
- Car (Lamborghini, Tesla, Ferrari or any other brand of car)
 - Food items (chocolate, coffee, or some other popular food item)
- Gasoline

Adam smith had very strong moral advice for capitalists. Smith is often credited as the founder of the system of capitalism. There are numerous historical examples of peoples practicing capitalistic principles prior to Smith, but western systems of education continue to promote Smith as the founder of capitalism. However, it is still important to analyze what Smith had to say about capitalism, especially its moral and ethical boundaries which are not highlighted in western schools of thought.

http://www.philosophersbeard.org/2011/10/recovering-adam-smiths-ethical.html

Smith's views on the problems of capitalism

Excerpts from the *Wealth of Nations:*

"To hurt in any degree the interest of any one order of citizens, for no other purpose but to promote that of some other, is evidently contrary to that justice and equality of treatment which the sovereign owes to all the different orders of his subjects."

"Every man, as long as he does not violate the laws of justice, is left perfectly free to pursue his own interest his own way, and to bring both his industry and capital into competition with those of any other man, or order of men." (WN IV.ix. 51).

From what you know of how capitalism works in the world, what is your opinion on its impact on people and the world? Does it observe the moral and ethical boundaries that Adam Smith advised? Explain.

The wealth and power accumulated by the United States was only possible due to its treatment of Native Americans and the forced enslavement of Africans. These two elements are the foundational building blocks of America capitalism. When is it right to steal land, resources, bodies, labor, break up families because your profits are more important? Explain.

To get a more tangible understanding of global capitalism complete the task on the website below.

slaveryfootprint.org

Include your results here:

What do your results tell you about how you participate in the global economic system? How do you feel about your results? What should be done about these results? Do you feel these results are in line with Smith's moral and ethical views on how capitalism should function? Explain.

If you're in a learning space with multiple learners, then compile the results of all learners to see how many people are impacted by our global economic system. How do you all feel about these results? Do you feel these results are in line with Smith's moral and ethical views on how capitalism should function? Explain.

"Black Child"

Black Child

Themes:

- Family

- Sacrifice (What you have to do for family. Especially what families do to prepare for the next generation)

- Protecting generations

Prerequisites and Scaffolding:

Treatment of children in different societies. Also, how the idea of a child is relative depending on place and time.

Children being protected by society or exploited for work by greater society. It's one thing to work for your family, it's another thing to have to work for capitalists.

Curriculum Implementation:

1. Initial Poem Reflection Learning Experience

2. Vocabulary Learning Experience

3. Second Poem Reflection Learning Experience

4. Unique Learning Experiences: Black Child

This chapter has one unique LE.

Learners will become familiar with some of the most egregious historic attacks on black children in this society. Making learners more familiar with how these children were treated by the society around them. It's a way to try to humanize their experience for the learners and then use that as a foundation point for exploring how black children and other minority children are treated in this society.

The LE continues with an analysis of how children are being treated in current society. The learners will compare current treatment of children with the United Nations Human Rights Convention of the Rights of the Child.

5. Deep Dive Poetry Analysis/Literary Device Learning Experience

6. Chapter Review Learning Experience

Expansion LEs:

Child labor laws in the USA and other parts of the world

Children tried as adults in other parts of the world

Black Child

Chronological and Spatial Thinking

Students compare the present with the past, evaluating the consequences of past events and decisions and determining the lessons that were learned.

Students analyze how change happens at different rates at different times; understand that some aspects can change while others remain the same; and understand that change is complicated and affects not only technology and politics but also values and beliefs.

Historical Research, Evidence, and Point of View

Students distinguish valid arguments from fallacious arguments in historical interpretations.

Students identify bias and prejudice in historical interpretations.

Students construct and test hypotheses; collect, evaluate, and employ information from multiple primary and secondary sources; and apply it in oral and written presentations.

Historical Interpretation

Students show the connections, causal and otherwise, between particular historical events and larger social, economic, and political trends and developments.

Students recognize the complexity of historical causes and effects, including the limitations on determining cause and effect.

Students interpret past events and issues within the context in which an event unfolded rather than solely in terms of present-day norms and values.

Students understand the meaning, implication, and impact of historical events and recognize that events could have taken other directions.

Standards and Learning objectives

1. Explain how demands of African Americans helped produce a stimulus for civil rights, including President Roosevelt's ban on racial discrimination in defense industries in 1941, and how African Americans' service in World War II produced a stimulus for President Truman's decision to end segregation in the armed forces in 1948.

2. Examine and analyze the key events, policies, and court cases in the evolution of civil rights, including Dred Scott v. Sandford, Plessy v. Ferguson, Brown v. Board of Education, Regents of the University of California v. Bakke, and California Proposition 209.

4. Examine the roles of civil rights advocates (e.g., A. Philip Randolph, Martin Luther King, Jr., Malcom X, Thurgood Marshall, James Farmer, Rosa Parks), including the significance of Martin Luther King, Jr.'s "Letter from Birmingham Jail" and "I Have a Dream" speech.

Discuss the diffusion of the civil rights movement of African Americans from the churches of the rural South and the urban North, including the resistance to racial desegregation in Little

Rock and Birmingham, and how the advances influenced the agendas, strategies, and effectiveness of the quests of American Indians, Asian Americans, and Hispanic Americans for civil rights and equal opportunities.

6. Analyze the passage and effects of civil rights and voting rights legislation (e.g., 1964 Civil Rights Act, Voting Rights Act of 1965) and the Twenty-Fourth Amendment, with an emphasis on equality of access to education and to the political process.

7. Analyze the women's rights movement from the era of Elizabeth Stanton and Susan Anthony and the passage of the Nineteenth Amendment to the movement launched in the 1960s, including differing perspectives on the roles of women.

Students analyze the major social problems and domestic policy issues in contemporary American society.

1. Discuss the reasons for the nation's changing immigration policy, with emphasis on how the Immigration Act of 1965 and successor acts have transformed American society.

3. Describe the changing roles of women in society as reflected in the entry of more women into the labor force and the changing family structure.

6. Analyze the persistence of poverty and how different analyses of this issue influence welfare reform, health insurance reform, and other social policies.

7. Explain how the federal, state, and local governments have responded to demographic and social changes such as population shifts to the suburbs, racial concentrations in the cities, Frostbelt-to-Sunbelt migration, international migration, decline of family farms, increases in out-of-wedlock births, and drug abuse.

Black Child (2015)

Black child, my child,
with all the sincerity I can muster
forming the most unbiased and humble opinion,
I say to you
that you are the envy of all of creation.

It is a universal fact that your genetic inheritance
is straight from the material that spawned civilization.

It was men and women in your blessed hue
who walked this planet first.

They pondered the realities of life on earth
and passed on their precious gifts to you.

When you stand in the power that you posses
the sun, the moon, the stars and everything upon the earth and in the heavens
feels that slight twinge of their heart strings,
as your elegance and grace is laid bare before them.

You are the personification of the highest definition of beauty.
Which is so sacred it is incapable of being spoken by a human tongue.
An anthropomorphic presentation of all that can be right in the world.
A noble embodiment of freedom and struggle.

You are love, and you are loved.

And I must apologize for the world that I have to bring you into.
Black child, my child
know that I have tried,
and others who are more worthy than me have tried with life and limb
to create a world that would not offend you.
It is a fact of this life that I must prepare you
for the evil that men do.

Black Child, my child
know that I have endeavored with every effort
to carve out a sliver of this world to place you in
where you will not be blemished or tarnished
by the venom and garbage
of heartless hardened men
who have yet to hearken
to the sweetness of your song.

They say ignorance is a state
which equates lack of knowledge or information.

Modern man is a woefully ignorant,
a penniless
indigent pauper.
Whose transactions are bankrupt.

For, If they listened, then they would know.
They would know the beauty that produced you
and is produced by you.
They would recognize the seed of the tree of knowledge
by its roots and its fruit.
They would be transformed by the lessons you have buried in your flesh.

Through knowing you they would know themselves.

But they reject,

they cover up,
wipe away,
smudge out.
Like a tantrum touting toddler claiming everything is mine.

Their hearts and souls become decrepit.
Blind and illiterate,
deaf by choice and
dumb with distinction.
All to protect the trivial trinkets of western adornment
they believe belong to them.

They believe these things make them more beautiful than you.
Spiritually and morally destitute and inept.
They are unable to feel the brail that is written in your soul.

This is how jealousy,
envy,
hubris and arrogance
have manifested in what could've been a great people.

May their example be a cautionary tale to you, Black Child.
Do not accept their ways as your own.
You were made to sing and dance in the sun.
The moon bore witness to your song.
The stars shine bright in tribute to your smile.
Black child, my child
never forget who and what you are.
This wisdom of the elders has been passed on for generations
since time immemorial and now I present it to you.

Many will attempt to change,
corrupt,

influence,
steal,
appropriate,
confuse,
challenge,
humiliate,
denigrate,
judge,
and hate you for being you.

This is part of your sentence as a Black Child,
but you must always know that you are
greater
than.

You are the first.

You are the fulcrum providing the balance
the universe rests upon.

The world is again waiting for you to assume your rightful position
of leader in the cosmos.

May we all live to see that day where you, Black Child
again lead us safely home.

Vocabulary Study Chart: "Black Child"

Word	Definition(s) and Synonym(s)	Copy the line or sentence from the text.	Your own example sentence
Personification			
Anthropomorphic			
Embodiment			
Hearken			

Word	Definition(s) and Synonym(s)	Copy the line or sentence from the text.	Your own example sentence
Indigent			
Pauper			
Trivial			
Trinkets			

Word	Definition(s) and Synonym(s)	Copy the line or sentence from the text.	Your own example sentence
Destitute			
Inept			
Hubris			
Immemorial			

Word	Definition(s) and Synonym(s)	Copy the line or sentence from the text.	Your own example sentence
Fulcrum			

Black Boy Poems Research Learning Experience

In the reflection section for the poem "Black Child" a number of specific historical references are mentioned. For each of the references provide a brief summary of what happened historically. In an attempt to humanize the child or children impacted you will also become more aware of their childhood context.

Personal Connection:

What rights and protections should be granted to children in our society?

What rights do children have in your society? What rights don't they have in your society? Use the United Nations Human Rights' Convention of the Rights of the Child as a resource.

Research Questions:

Pick one of these topics to research and answer the research questions.

-George Junius Stinney Jr.

-Bombing of Birmingham church,

-Bombing of MOVE

Age:

What was the popular music for youth of that time?

Popular toys/games/films in the community for youth at that time?

What grade(s) would they have been in? What school were they attending?

How tall were they, or do you think they were for their age?

Contemporary and local analysis

How are children being treated in the area you live in? How are children who have been admitted to the foster system being treated? List the demographics of the children in the "system".

How many children are in juvenile facilities in your area? What age can children be tried as an adult in your state? What are the demographics of the children in your area that are tried as an adult?

How much is spent on the education of children in your state? Does the amount spent on children for education change based on the color of the students? Explain the difference if one exists.

How many children in your home state are homeless? How many are without access to quality food and healthcare?

Response and analysis

Do you believe all children are treated fairly in our society? Explain your answer. Give examples to support your belief.

In your opinion what are some of the most important issues in our current society that have an impact on children? What do you believe should be done about those issues? Explain.

Black Boy Poems Curriculum

"Death Toll"

Death Toll

Themes:

Righteous Anger - there are things we should be angry about and healthy ways to exercise that anger.

Black Death. Society's disregard of death and victimization of specific populations.

Social media and its "viewer" persona. Through social media we are exposed to so much information. So of that is prevalence of black death.

Social media culture of observing black death without doing something about it. Observing atrocities and then continuing to scroll through our timeline to something else without taking steps outside of a post or hashtag to do something about those issues in our world.

Prerequisites and Scaffolding:

- Eric Garner (choked)

- Sam Dubose (shot by Cincinnati cop)

- Sandra Bland (ped-zone)

- John Crawford III (Walmart)

- AME - Dylan Rouf

- Strange Fruit - Billie Holliday

- Tree of Liberty - Thomas Jefferson quote but the blood that refreshes the "liberty" of some is the blood of indigenous and black folks.

- Stepin Fetchit

Curriculum Implementation:

1. Initial Poem Reflection Learning Experience

2. Vocabulary Learning Experience

3. Second Poem Reflection Learning Experience

4. Unique Learning Experiences: Death Toll

This chapter has two unique LEs.

This LE allows the learners to explore the military industrial complex of the USA. They are also asked to share their thoughts and opinions on rules of engagement when fighting occurs. The LE pushes them to analyze language of "war" and the phrasing of conflict critically using UN and Geneva convention documents/ definitions.

The second LE is a historical analysis of exclusion and inclusion. This will require the learners to analyze the groups who have been historically disenfranchised by colonial and constitutional America and their path to "inclusion".

5. Deep Dive Poetry Analysis/Literary Device Learning Experience

6. Chapter Review Learning Experience

Expansion LEs:

The price of war. Who benefits in our current context from the death and destruction of other peoples and places? What is the impact of war/state violence/murder on the peoples who are experiencing it?

Death Toll

Chronological and Spatial Thinking

Students compare the present with the past, evaluating the consequences of past events and decisions and determining the lessons that were learned.

Students analyze how change happens at different rates at different times; understand that some aspects can change while others remain the same; and understand that change is complicated and affects not only technology and politics but also values and beliefs.

Students relate current events to the physical and human characteristics of places and regions.

Historical Research, Evidence, and Point of View

Students distinguish valid arguments from fallacious arguments in historical interpretations.

Students identify bias and prejudice in historical interpretations.

Students evaluate major debates among historians concerning alternative interpretations of the past, including an analysis of authors' use of evidence and the distinctions between sound generalizations and misleading oversimplifications.

Students construct and test hypotheses; collect, evaluate, and employ information from multiple primary and secondary sources; and apply it in oral and written presentations.

Historical Interpretation

Students show the connections, causal and otherwise, between particular historical events and larger social, economic, and political trends and developments.

Students recognize the complexity of historical causes and effects, including the limitations on determining cause and effect.

Students interpret past events and issues within the context in which an event unfolded rather than solely in terms of present-day norms and values.

Students understand the meaning, implication, and impact of historical events and recognize that events could have taken other directions.

Standards and Learning objectives

Analyze the philosophy of government expressed in the Declaration of Independence, with an emphasis on government as a means of securing individual rights (e.g., key phrases such as "all men are created equal, that they are endowed by their Creator with certain unalienable Rights").

1. List the original aims of Reconstruction and describe its effects on the political and social structures of different regions.

2. Identify the push-pull factors in the movement of former slaves to the cities in the North and to the West and their differing experiences in those regions (e.g., the experiences of Buffalo Soldiers).

3. Understand the effects of the Freedmen's Bureau and the restrictions placed on the rights and opportunities of freedmen, including racial segregation and "Jim Crow" laws.

4. Trace the rise of the Ku Klux Klan and describe the Klan's effects.

5. Understand the Thirteenth, Fourteenth, and Fifteenth Amendments to the Constitution and analyze their connection to Reconstruction.

Death toll (2015)

I once said before,
"We hold each breath close
like Uncle Sam holds
political prisoners on death row.
He scared to let go,
he fears the power
of the child of the ghetto."

But this death toll
is at my threshold,
and if you didn't know
this being black in America ish is stressful.

Never knowing what's gonna happen when you set forth
or you step forth from your front porch.
Maybe that's the reason
why I'm contemplating death more.

Like

what's it gonna feel like when my flesh cold
and they put my body in that fresh hole,
and I hate being so necro
but negroes and death go
hand in hand
like young kids back in the day who used to thumb wrestle.

That Grim Reaper be on our back like an echo,
echo,
echo,
echo.

I've seen police choke a nigga until his breath go.

I seen them point that glock at his top
cock back that shot
and then let go.

Cop must've thought he had a bulletproof dome like Destro.
The boy had locks with a front license plate in the glove box,
so tell me what he dead for.

I seen them arrest a sister for failing to signal
while driving through a Ped-Zone.
Should've been a citation
still they took her to jail

and 3 days later she dead though.
And they think that we stupid enough to believe
that suicide is the reason why we putting flowers on her headstone.

I seen them shoot a man shopping at Walmart
for an air rifle outside of Dayton Metro.
Cops magically appear on the scene
with guns out like presto.
Shots get fired while he looking at them "Falling Price" specials.
Now he at the morgue under a white sheet
with a tag on his left toe.

That's death toll!

These American streets are a morbid expo
of lifeless black bodies lying exposed.
And they quick to be on some, "oh no, this ain't that retro Jim Crow."
But we know this that new version
2.0
Michelle Alexander said so.

This here is my manifesto.

We sick and tried of dying.
We putting an end to dying.
Either by our hands
or the hands of this white violence.
And I know I have agency
over this hate in me,
but I experience a little bit of latency
when I think about that white boy
and them 9 that he killed at the AME.
You can look at my face and see
black rage in the place to be.
What you expect
when y'all doing this so blatantly?

My country, tis of thee

you have made me a strange and bitter fruit
which you harvest from your tree of liberty.

And those roots are buried deep beneath the soil,
four hundred years of this racial terrorism and turmoil.
Better be careful before this melting pot start to boil.

But you are not equipped with empathy.
You do not posses the capacity to change.
You are so thoroughly programmed

that you do not understand the error of your ways.
And my people have changed.
This is not that docile
hat in hand
Stepin Fetchit
step to the side.
We that Wretched of the Earth,
with a ratchet tucked,
West Side til I die.
And we already accustomed to dying for no reason.
And once these lines remove the poison
and blindfolds from my people's minds
whose favorite past time is killing their own kind,
they gonna want to get even.

So what does this mean for America as a whole?
Keep killing my people, stealing those that we love from our homes,
and you're going to leave us with no other choice
but to show America the true definition of a Death Toll.

Vocabulary Study Chart: "Death Toll"

Word	Definition(s) and Synonym(s)	Copy the line or sentence from the text.	Your own example sentence
Necro			
Manifesto			
Agency			
Latency			

Word	Definition(s) and Synonym(s)	Copy the line or sentence from the text.	Your own example sentence
Docile			

Black Boy Poems Research Learning Experience

The poem "Death Toll" ends with Tyson issuing a warning to western civilization, "if you keep killing our people, stealing those that we love from our homes, then you'll leave us with no choice but to show America the true definition of a death toll."

Knowledge Connection:

In the history of conflict between peoples a concept has evolved that is sometimes referred to as "just war." Do you believe there is such a thing as a just war? If so, then what makes something a just war? If not, then why do you feel it doesn't exist?

Is it ever right to fight? If so, then when is it right to fight? If not, then why is it never right to fight?

Since war/fighting does exist in our contemporary society what do you believe should be the rules of engagement when peoples/nations fight? Provide a brief description of what you believe should be "permissible" in a conflict. Compare your thoughts with Geneva Conventions articles (51-55)

https://ihl-databases.icrc.org/ihl/WebART/470-750065

https://ihl-databases.icrc.org/applic/ihl/ihl.nsf/ART/470-750067?OpenDocument

https://ihl-databases.icrc.org/applic/ihl/ihl.nsf/ART/470-750068?OpenDocument

https://ihl-databases.icrc.org/applic/ihl/ihl.nsf/ART/470-750069?OpenDocument

https://ihl-databases.icrc.org/applic/ihl/ihl.nsf/ART/470-750070?OpenDocument

Building an understanding of context

How much does the United States spend on its military per year? Compare that with money spent on education and social services. What are your thoughts about the differences in budgetary spending?

How many armed conflicts is the United States currently involved in throughout the world? How many countries does the United States have a military presence in? What justifications is the United States using for its armed campaigns?

The vernacular of "modern day warfare" is filled with dualistic concepts of patriots/terrorists, soldiers/enemy combatants and good/evil. In your opinion what is the difference between a "patriot" and a "terrorist"? Explain. What is the difference between a "soldier" and an "enemy combatant"? Explain

Definitions of Terrorism

UN Security Council - *"criminal acts, including against civilians, committed with the intent to cause death or serious bodily injury, or taking of hostages, with the purpose to provoke a state of terror in the general public or in a group of persons or particular persons, intimidate a population or compel a government or an international organization to do or to abstain from doing any act, which constitute offenses within the scope of and as defined in the international conventions and protocols relating to terrorism, are under no circumstances justifiable by considerations of a political, philosophical, ideological, racial, ethnic, religious or other similar nature."*

NATO (2014) *"The unlawful use or threatened use of force or violence against individuals or property in an attempt to coerce or intimidate governments or societies to achieve political, religious or ideological objectives."*

European colonization of the Western Hemisphere was only possible due to the violence and warfare colonial powers visited upon various indigenous populations. In your opinion, were the colonizers justified in using violence to take control of people, lands and resources from the indigenous natives? Explain your answer.

One of the most important freedom struggles took place between the French Empire and the forcibly enslaved population of Haiti between 1791-1804. Briefly research the history of the Haitian revolution. Based on your research what were the justifications the various parities involved gave for their fight? Do you feel any of the parties were right in the decisions they made to deal with that conflict? Explain.

In the history of the United States hat organization is known on record as the oldest terrorist group? When did they start and what were their reasons for forming? In what ways have they been responsible for destruction of property and loss of life? If rooting out terrorism is such an important priority for US society, then why do you feel this organization is still able to operate in our society? What are some current examples of acts of "terrorism" perpetrated by members of this group?

https://en.wikipedia.org/wiki/History_of_terrorism#The_United_States

Black Boy Poems Research Learning Experience

Historical analysis of exclusion and inclusion.

Personal Connection:

What rights are you aware of that are extended to you in your daily life?

What rights do you feel should be extended to all members of our society?

Are there any groups in our society right now that you feel are not granted the same access to these rights? Explain who and why.

Context for Research

At the founding of this country there were at least three marginalized groups. Their experiences <u>were not the same</u>, but they all were not granted equal access to rights and privileges in society. Those groups were (**Indigenous/Native Americans**, **Black People** and **Women**). Analyze two foundational texts of the United States of America. (**Declaration of Independence** and **The Constitution of the United States**) Examine how these groups are represented in these documents.

Questions to answer:

Who wrote the document? What demographics of society do they represent? Do you believe their demographic(s) might have biased how they drafted these documents? Explain.

Were any of the historically excluded groups included in the drafting of these documents? In what ways were these groups included or excluded in the context of the documents? Quote lines from those texts that reference those groups and then write a response to the lines.

When were these groups legally "included" into the greater society? What serves as example of this inclusion?

Critical Thinking:

Do you feel it is possible for a group that has been historically excluded by this society to eventually be fully included? Explain your answer. If you believe they can be included, then explain how or what steps have been taken to include them. If you believe it is not possible, then elaborate on the reason(s) why you believe they won't ever be fully included.

What other groups have been institutionally excluded/discriminated against in US society? Provide examples of that exclusion. How are these groups being treated in society today?

What other groups in today's society are currently being excluded? Explain who they are and what seems to be the rationale for excluding them from society?

Black Boy Poems Curriculum

"You"

You

Themes:

- The black experience in the south and the black experience in other parts of the USA.

- Power of women.

- The divergent experience of black women from white women in the USA.

- Richard Wright

Prerequisites and Scaffolding:

- Nina Simone - Mississippi Goddam

- Frantz Ferdinand

- The harshness of Mississippi on black people

- Mississippi was the state with the greatest number of lynchings

- Cicely Tyson (my namesake)

- Richard Wright's work and impact

Curriculum Implementation:

1. Initial Poem Reflection Learning Experience
2. Vocabulary Learning Experience
3. Second Poem Reflection Learning Experience
4. Unique Learning Experiences: You

This chapter has two unique LEs.

The first LE allows the learners to examine the history of Mississippi.

The second LE looks at the great migrations from Mississippi. Learners will be asked to compare the great migrations from the south with other peoples who have been forced to migrate from their homes.

5. Deep Dive Poetry Analysis/Literary Device Learning Experience

6. Chapter Review Learning Experience

Expansion LEs:

Response to Nina Simone's Mississippi Goddam

Current analysis of black life in Mississippi

You

Chronological and Spatial Thinking

Students compare the present with the past, evaluating the consequences of past events and decisions and determining the lessons that were learned.

Students analyze how change happens at different rates at different times; understand that some aspects can change while others remain the same; and understand that change is complicated and affects not only technology and politics but also values and beliefs.

Students use a variety of maps and documents to interpret human movement, including major patterns of domestic and international migration, changing environmental preferences and settlement patterns, the frictions that develop between population groups, and the diffusion of ideas, technological innovations, and goods.

Students relate current events to the physical and human characteristics of places and regions.

Historical Research, Evidence, and Point of View

Students distinguish valid arguments from fallacious arguments in historical interpretations.

Students identify bias and prejudice in historical interpretations.

Students evaluate major debates among historians concerning alternative interpretations of the past, including an analysis of authors' use of evidence and the distinctions between sound generalizations and misleading oversimplifications.

Students construct and test hypotheses; collect, evaluate, and employ information from multiple primary and secondary sources; and apply it in oral and written presentations.

Historical Interpretation

Students show the connections, causal and otherwise, between particular historical events and larger social, economic, and political trends and developments.

Students recognize the complexity of historical causes and effects, including the limitations on determining cause and effect.

Students interpret past events and issues within the context in which an event unfolded rather than solely in terms of present-day norms and values.

Students understand the meaning, implication, and impact of historical events and recognize that events could have taken other directions.

Standards and Learning objectives

Students analyze human modifications of landscapes and examine the resulting environmental policy issues.

3. Outline the major treaties with American Indian nations during the administrations of the first four presidents and the varying outcomes of those treaties.

Discuss the influence of industrialization and technological developments on the region, including human modification of the landscape and how physical geography shaped human actions (e.g., growth of cities, deforestation, farming, mineral extraction).

1. Describe the development of the agrarian economy in the South, identify the locations of the cotton-producing states, and discuss the significance of cotton and the cotton gin.

2. Trace the origins and development of slavery; its effects on black Americans and on the region's political, social, religious, economic, and cultural development; and identify the strategies that were tried to both overturn and preserve it (e.g., through the writings and historical documents on Nat Turner, Denmark Vesey).

3. Examine the characteristics of white Southern society and how the physical environment influenced events and conditions prior to the Civil War.

4. Compare the lives of and opportunities for free blacks in the North with those of free blacks in the South.

You (2009)

Where swamp waters flow
and fat mosquitos fly.
A young daughter grows
around where them gators lay.
It's black magic,
mathematics,
lots casted
cowry shells,
chicken blood
putting roots up on the slave master.
Where you might see a black man hung up on them branches.
Where we close to, homie,
man, I think we close to Natchez.
It's that dirty dirty
share cropping,
cotton picking,
bright and early
lashes on our back and our flesh is burning.

I see her in an old faded picture
her soul plated with scripture.
Her skin light and face tight
because of the mixture
of the slave master who made em suffer,
and her native brother,
and the blood that come from the land of her mother.
It all runs through her veins.
No more shackles because freedom came.
Grandma Dolly was her name.
The next generation came
when the century changed over.
My Great Gram saw the world go to war over Franz Ferdinand.
Color like a rubber band holding us back.
That's something my folks in the South can understand.
If you black you wasn't viewed as a man.
My great gram was light,
couldn't pass
still viewed
as second class citizen.
Passed down through my lineage,
Essie May my Grandma
born in Meridian.
Around the Great Depression.
Jim Crow stole our innocence.
Left us with bitterness.
Moms keep your sons at home
because outside they lynching men.

Grandma was witness to it
because she was living through it.
Separate but equal schooling.
Strange fruit
seeing her classmates strung up in them nooses.
A nightmare
but it's real life.
She met up with a man who made her feel like
the sky's the limit.
But he playing both sides of the fences.
My grandma pregnant with my mom he ain't trying to listen.
So she started living
for her daughter,
tried to make sure that she got more than everything she was given
in the delta of Mississippi.
My mom was young and pretty.
Her pops was never there
he everywhere with other women in the city.
Left her for her moms to raise.
She a single black mom looking at harder days.
She worked odd jobs trying to put food on my momma's plate.
But it ain't easy for her many times she thought she break.
Meet another young man so she thinking she safe,
she didn't know he type to flip out once he get a taste,
and that liquor get in his system.
My moms would pay attention,
she dreamed of one day raising a young man who would be different.
So everyday in her womb I would sit and listen
to her tell me about my mission.
She said, "you!"

It was a cold night in November
the sign of the Scorpio.
Her younger brother died just a year before from overdose.
My birth brought life back to a family that trying to cope,
she held me close and filled my ears with hope.
And she named her boy Tyson after the actress Cicely,
before I spoke in poetry
my momma already envisioned great things in store for me.
Now I'm living out my destiny doing my best to be
everything that she wanted for me.
She told me to stand strong,
she told me to shine.
She told me respect women at each and all times.
She told me God buried something great in me deep inside
and that the world gets to hear it every time I speak a rhyme.
She said, "you!"

Vocabulary Study Chart: "You"

Word	Definition(s) and Synonym(s)	Copy the line or sentence from the text.	Your own example sentence
Plated			
Homage			
Lineage			
Inkling			

Word	Definition(s) and Synonym(s)	Copy the line or sentence from the text.	Your own example sentence
Catalyst			
Paragon			
Rife			
Diabolical			

Word	Definition(s) and Synonym(s)	Copy the line or sentence from the text.	Your own example sentence
Progeny			
Quarter (mass noun)			

Black Boy Poems Research Learning Experience

Mississippi is an important character in *Black Boy Poems* because it is the home state of one of Tyson Amir's favorite writers, Richard Wright; and home to at least 4 generations of Tyson's family on his mother's side. This LE will allow learners to become more acquainted with the history and legacy of Mississippi.

Knowledge Connection/Context Building

What is the current population and demographics of Mississippi? Where does Mississippi rank in terms of wealth compared with other states in the US? What was Mississippi's wealth as a state prior to the beginning of the Civil War?

What is the wealthiest state in the United States today? How does it rank among other global economies?

History of Mississippi (Historical Context)

What indigenous populations lived in Mississippi before European colonization? What were some characteristics of their culture and people?

When did they first began to encounter European colonization? Who came and what was the outcome of the interaction between the European colonizers and the indigenous population of Mississippi?

When did Mississippi become a "territory" of the United States? (potential resource)

When did Mississippi become a state in the union? What was the population of "free" and forcibly enslaved people at the start of the Civil War?

Where were the richest people in Mississippi prior to the Civil War?

How much of the global cotton market was the United States responsible for prior to the Civil War? How much of that cotton crop came from Mississippi?

During reconstruction and the period referred to as Jim Crow, Mississippi was known for its racist laws and climate/culture of terror and violence directed at blacks. What are some examples of racist laws/policies enacted in Mississippi? Give some examples of the violence black people experienced in Mississippi during this era.

How does Mississippi rank today in terms of education, health, life expectancy, employment and average income per resident based on racial demographics? What do you think is the cause of the major statistical differences between racial groups in Mississippi? Explain.

Black Boy Poems Research Learning Experience

Forced Migration

For years Black people tried to flee the oppressive conditions that Mississippi forced them to endure. This led to multiple mass forced migrations from Mississippi to other parts of the United States and world. We currently live in a time where multiple communities are being forced to migrate from their homes due to a variety of social, environmental, economic and political reasons.

Forced Migration/Voluntary and Involuntary Migration

In this history of colonial and constitutional America two populations have been forced into numerous migrations, Indigenous Natives and Black People. Colonization and western expansion has constantly forced Indigenous populations off their ancestral lands. The forced removal from the African continent of Black peoples began their forced migration patterns due to theft. Once brought to colonial and constitutional America many black people sought freedom by escaping their forced servitude. Some attempted to travel as far north as possible. Others fled south to Spanish held territories. Some even fled to Mexico.

How many blacks left the south in the first and second waves of migration? Where did folks migrate, and what were the major motivating factors for these migrations? Where did most of these people migrate? How were black folks treated in the new areas they arrived in?

How many Native Americans were forced to leave their ancestral homelands due to Western Colonization? Where were they forced to move to? What are the conditions on the lands where they now reside?

Compare and contrast these migration patterns with Central American migration in the later part of the 20th century and early part of the 21st century? Why were folks fleeing their homes? What were the push/pull factors impacting their migration? How were these migrants treated upon arrival to the USA? Was the USA complicit in creating the conditions in their homeland that motivated their migration? (Resource)

What other communities are being forced to migrate from their homelands in today's society? What are the reasons why they are being forced to flee? Where are these groups now attempting to relocate to? Are they being welcomed in the new areas they are trying to migrate to? Explain your answers.

Black Boy Poems Research Learning Experience

The majority of this poem takes place in Mississippi which has the infamous distinction of being the wealthiest and most brutal state during the first iteration of forced slavery. European colonization and the colonial empires these countries built were only possible due to their use of white supremacist predatory capitalism. In this LE we'll examine the capitalistic and colonial goals behind different eras of White colonization.

Knowledge connection

What have you been taught about the connections between capitalism and European colonization? Based on what you know, in what ways are they connected? What impact has capitalism and colonization had on peoples and the planet?

_____

_____

_____

_____

Response to Adam Smith quote

"No society can surely be flourishing and happy, of which the far greater part of the members are poor and miserable."

_____

_____

_____

_____

Response to Karl Marx quote

"Accumulation of wealth at one pole is at the same time accumulation of misery, agony of toil, slavery, ignorance, brutality, mental degradation, at the opposite pole."

_____

_____

_____

_____

Analysis of wealth in today's society

Global:

Who are the wealthiest people in the world, and how much are they worth? What industries did they get their money from?

What are some of the "poorest" countries in the world, and how much are they worth? If they were colonized, who were the colonial powers that took control of these countries?

Local:

What is the average income in your city?

What is the poverty level in your city, and how many people are considered at or below the poverty level?

Average price for a house and rent.

Average price for college and university.

Average amount of debt people have in your city, state and country? Here's a great resource to share on income inequality.

What does wealth inequality look like in terms of skin color/"race"? How much of the new wealth that's generated in the economic system goes to the wealthy and the poor?

Based on the quotes from Marx and Smith and the data you collected from the previous questions, how is capitalism working for the majority of the people in your national and local context? How is it working for the majority of the people in our global context?

_____

_____

_____

_____

What do you feel should be done about these economic conditions which continue to become more and more extreme everyday? What changes if any do you feel should be made to our global economic system? How should those changes be implemented?

_____

_____

_____

_____

Extra resources:

https://www.theguardian.com/global-development/2017/jan/16/worlds-eight-richest-people-have-same-wealth-as-poorest-50

https://www.scmp.com/news/world/united-states-canada/article/2119052/three-richest-people-us-own-much-wealth-bottom-half

https://www.telegraph.co.uk/business/2018/01/22/forty-two-people-hold-wealth-half-world-oxfam-says/

https://www.oxfam.org/en/pressroom/pressreleases/2017-01-16/just-8-men-own-same-wealth-half-world

https://www.youtube.com/watch?v=QPKKQnijnsM&t=9s

Ideas to explore more:

- Lands being exploited for natural resources
- The history of British industrialization and textile industry
- King cotton and how at one point in time it was considered more valuable than gold.
- Transportation and the natural resources necessary for our transportation infrastructure to exist.
- The role of oil in extracting, manufacturing and distributing consumer goods and technologies
- How data is now being described as the "new oil". (Surveillance Capitalism)

"_A Poem for Mario_"

A Poem for Mario

Themes:

Societal and media bias when white people are the perpetrators of violence.

What can be called the triple death of black life in media and society. The person is assassinated in body, character and often times in the justice system because no one is held accountable for their murder.

Prerequisites and Scaffolding:

Ways to analyze societal and media bias:

The Doll Study: How black and white is viewed in society

https://www.youtube.com/watch?v=DYCz1ppTjiM&t=13s

https://www.youtube.com/watch?v=EQACkg5i4AY

How White and Black are treated in society

https://www.youtube.com/watch?v=fTcSVQJ2h8g

https://youtu.be/HGJMgCn0fQs

Another example of media bias in their representation of a black victim.

https://www.washingtonpost.com/news/morning-mix/wp/2018/07/26/critics-say-the-media-makes-innocent-blacks-look-dangerous-heres-their-latest-example/?utm_term=.5aa07517011a

Curriculum Implementation:

1. Initial Poem Reflection Learning Experience

2. Vocabulary Learning Experience

3. Second Poem Reflection Learning Experience

4. Unique Learning Experiences: A Poem for Mario

This chapter has one unique LE.

This LE is a comparison between the portrayal of both Mario Woods and Robert Lewis Dear Jr. in the media. Learners will be directed to different sources published right around the

5. Deep Dive Poetry Analysis/Literary Device Learning Experience

6. Chapter Review Learning Experience

Expansion LEs:

Investigation of how many times officers have been held accountable for killings of black bodies and other people murdered by police.

A Poem for Mario

Chronological and Spatial Thinking

Students compare the present with the past, evaluating the consequences of past events and decisions and determining the lessons that were learned.

Students analyze how change happens at different rates at different times; understand that some aspects can change while others remain the same; and understand that change is complicated and affects not only technology and politics but also values and beliefs.

Historical Research, Evidence, and Point of View

Students identify bias and prejudice in historical interpretations.

Students construct and test hypotheses; collect, evaluate, and employ information from multiple primary and secondary sources; and apply it in oral and written presentations.

Historical Interpretation

Students show the connections, causal and otherwise, between particular historical events and larger social, economic, and political trends and developments.

Students recognize the complexity of historical causes and effects, including the limitations on determining cause and effect.

Students interpret past events and issues within the context in which an event unfolded rather than solely in terms of present-day norms and values.

Students evaluate and take and defend positions on the influence of the media on American political life.

Standards and Learning objectives

1. Discuss the meaning and importance of a free and responsible press.

2. Describe the roles of broadcast, print, and electronic media, including the Internet, as means of communication in American politics.

3. Explain how public officials use the media to communicate with the citizenry and to shape public opinion.

A Poem For Mario (2016)

I see him.
In my mind's eye he still sits
in that same place.
He a young black face
tucked in the back of the class.
He's quiet,
not the type to cat off
and laugh as time pass.
He's busy trying to master his own path.
I see the pain inside.
I see he don't want to remain inside.
I see the brain inside.
At times he'd raise his hand high to share some of his insight.
I see he gets it.
I see the boy,
he's young, black and gifted.
And We both know our blackness
leaves us trapped in the system.
He's gotta date, he's gonna hit those gates soon.
A new start,
motivated by the promises he made to his momma that he keeps in his heart.
He's a good dude,
be he ain't perfect.
Truthfully, none of us are,
and as far as the word go,
may he who is without sin cast the first stone.
There won't be any rocks flying,
but on that day them shots were flying,
like a firing squad who wouldn't stop
until he dropped and was dying.
Hearts dropped and broke and couldn't stop crying.
His folks shocked as I am
trying to calm that violence that rising inside them.
And I know this shouldn't be a eulogy keynote.
I should be standing, smiling right beside him,
watching him walk off with his diploma a brighter future on the horizon.

But you and I are only left to think of what might have been.

Momma Woods lost a son,
others lost a family member or a friend.
Me, I lost a student.
May we never lose our love for him.
May we never lose our hope that we will win.
And his leaving us will not be in vain, for we will make sure this never happens again.

Rest in Power and Peace, Mario. Justice for Mario Woods

Vocabulary Study Chart: "A Poem for Mario"

Word	Definition(s) and Synonym(s)	Copy the line or sentence from the text.	Your own example sentence
Eulogy			
Succumb			
Recidivism			
Ameliorate			

Word	Definition(s) and Synonym(s)	Copy the line or sentence from the text.	Your own example sentence
Christened			
Impunity			
Invective			
Epithets			

Word	Definition(s) and Synonym(s)	Copy the line or sentence from the text.	Your own example sentence
Corrosive			
Environs			
Connoting			
Indictments			

Word	Definition(s) and Synonym(s)	Copy the line or sentence from the text.	Your own example sentence
Parry			
Infallible			
Hippocratic oath			

Black Boy Poems Research Learning Experience

On 12/2/2015 in San Francisco, CA. Mario Woods, a former student of mine was brutally murdered by SFPD. Summarize the details of what happened to Mario Woods on 12/2.

On 11/27/2015 Robert Lewis Dear Jr. committed a terrorist attack on an abortion clinic and engaged in a gun battle with police officers. Summarize the details of what motivated the actions of Robert Lewis Dear Jr. and what happened to him in his interactions with police.

Compare and contrast Mario and Robert Lewis Dear Jr.'s experience with law enforcement?

Compare and contrast the depictions of Mario Woods and Robert Lewis Dear Jr.'s in news articles.

What do you feel contributes to the continued use of violence and force by law enforcement agents that largely impacts people of color, specifically black people? Use evidence from the articles to justify your opinion. (resource 1) (resource 2)

Articles written right after Mario was murdered:

https://sanfrancisco.cbslocal.com/2015/12/03/mario-woods-stabbing-suspect-killed-sfpd-confrontation-caught-on-video-san-francisco/

http://time.com/4151979/mario-woods-shooting-san-francisco/

Articles on Robert Lewis Dear:

https://www.nbcnews.com/news/us-news/who-robert-dear-planned-parenthood-shooting-suspect-seemed-strange-not-n470896

https://www.cbsnews.com/news/colorado-springs-shooting-robert-lewis-dear-neighbors-planned-parenthood-attack/

Articles on SFPD

https://www.sfchronicle.com/bayarea/article/SFPD-s-texting-scandal-Court-rules-officers-12955853.php

https://www.nbcbayarea.com/news/local/SFPD-Dropping-30-Cases-Daily-Amid-Due-to-Lab-Scandal-88551702.html

https://www.nytimes.com/2011/03/10/us/10narcs.html

https://abc7news.com/news/whistleblower-sfpd-crime-lab-scandal-dates-back-years/635644/

https://www.sfgate.com/crime/article/Ex-SFPD-Sgt-Ian-Furminger-gets-prison-for-6096649.php
Recent article on Mario woods

https://www.theguardian.com/us-news/2018/may/24/san-francisco-police-shooting-mario-woods-luis-gongora-no-charges

Literary Device Tool Kit

Black Boy Poems Poetry Analysis Learning Experience

Literary Devices, Poetic Terms & Lyrical Techniques

Here are a few examples of some of my favorite literary devices/techniques. These are tools that I don't intentionally use but they appear a lot in my work. Before compiling this list I couldn't name all of these devices. I know how to use them well but knowing how to name them isn't the same as knowing how to use them in your writing. I hope this tool kit will allow us to gain a better understanding of what some of us do intuitively, and allow us to better identify and define ways that we use language.

1. <u>Alliteration:</u> the repetition of the same sound usually at the beginning of a word.

Example: Moorish Science

"the epitome of a real emcee/lineage live in me/liberating them literally/with lyrical liturgies..."

This is one of my favorite techniques. A common use for alliteration is emphasis of a specific point or for more advanced writers/rhymers displaying a certain level of skill/ability in writing. Alliteration is common in everyday speech as well. You'll find alliteration in a lot of writings, especially in rap lyrics. A great number of rappers, emcees, and poets use alliteration in their work.

2. <u>Assonance:</u> the repetition of vowel sounds. Assonance can appear in hip hop lyrics with repetition of vowel sound word endings in a rhyme scheme.

Example: Khalil Shaheed

The effort is effortless/a poetical specialist/rhyme inspired by the world the flow is impressionist/ the mind's revolutionary soul is a separatist/most of my colleagues in this game ego at deficit/ they wanna battle instead of building so devilish/ ain't nothing wrong with trying represent your excellence/ but how we benefit berating and belittling men over these beats y'all gotta tell me what the message is/ the flow it be pessimist/ leaving us desolate/ we on the precipice of showing y'all that next ish/ no prerequisites needed/ what we spitting is freedom the exodus/ and this tradition is a testament/ elevating the best of us/ it's why we grind from the bottom of the sediment/ and see these lines that I rhyme combine our minds into a regiment/ and five fingers form a fist and break through impediments/ in case you needed evidence/ the flow is blessed by the beneficent/ infused with medicine so let us in/ I be your dedicated delegate/ to help us conquer our nemesis with some eloquence.

In this verse I use assonance to emphasize a rhyme scheme. Every rhyme has the e/i vowel sound repeated. I added more than just the repetition of the vowel sound but the rhyme wouldn't be possible without the assonance. The assonance is also coupled with a multi syllable rhyme. I enjoy the challenge of using the same rhyme ending and attempting to impart a message. I see it as a literary challenge when I'm writing to do an entire scheme with the same ending or assonance.

3. **Anthropomorphism** - taking an object, concept or something else that is not human and presenting it in a human form, or with human characteristics/qualities. This can also be very similar to personification. The idea of granting human qualities or characteristics to something that's not human.

Example: A Little Sunshine

… but we crave blood and in turn return more pain/ the language of the beast is where pain is the way to gain peace/ bomb civilians to the stone-age/ then black others of terror when the real problem is homemade/ O say, can you see/ that I Tyson have never been free/ a descendant of slaves/dodging bombs on Osage Ave./ In Philly in 85/Lady liberty ain't colorblind/ ain't seen no progress so its hard pressed for you to find…

(taking the concept of "liberty" and making it a person. The idea of Lady Liberty is a very common cultural phrase that is also an example of anthropomorphism. I then take it a step further in the anthropomorphism by saying the image of liberty as someone who is helping to call people to freedom is not true because she's only seeing a path to freedom for folks who aren't people of color.

4. **Circumlocution:** - the use of extra words to describe something that can be said in a more concise way, or with fewer/more direct wording.

Example: Praise be (I'll use this example again for Imagery)

From a clot of congealed blood, sperm cell to the ovary/
My conception pure poetry/ written before/Words would ever pour/
from my lips/ anointed/ my cup runneth over with blessings/ appointed/
To speak these poignant/ prose on microphones/
Raised where the rose grows/ through concrete floors/And natural fo-liage/
locked behind walls of metal and steel cold/To the touch/
windows to the heaven blocked by soot, smut, fog/ poisonous smog/
clogging the lungs of young ones./ God is an emblem/
which hangs around necks on chain in city slums./ Metallic birds of prey/
with machine gun talons/ hover eclipsing the sun/
It's chaotic where I'm from/ Pharaonic numbskulls in power/ got my bredren/
dead men/ walking to military drum *rolls for crumbs molded over/ soldiers of
misfortune rolling over in their grave...

-Circumlocution is a fun way of allowing the writer to use more words to express
a concept that can be described more directly. In the above example I take a few
concepts and intentionally word them in non-traditional ways. In the first line I use
circumlocution to describe the process of birth. Instead of saying I was born, I
say from a clot of congealed blood, sperm cell to the ovary...

-There's also a powerful example of assonance focused on the vowel sound "o"
in this piece.

5. __Double and Triple Entendre__ - words or phrases that can have multiple
meanings depending on the context used to understand the words/phrases. This
is a very popular technique in spoken word and hip hop lyrics. It also is a concept
that really demonstrates a mastery of the hip hop skill set and illustrates the
intellectual ability of the writer.

Example: Make it fast

*I spend time trying to defy the norm/like the time Jesus was born/formed/ with no
semen/**conceptually spit immaculate phrases**/when most rap pages/are filled
with dreams of Cadillac escalades/sitting on blades with/TVs in the headrest/**it's
the same old same cats chasing dirt until they're placed in a grave**/my soul
flirt with disaster/I escape to a cave/to gain solitude listen to my heart beat and
speak/cause on them streets it's so hard to eat and think/I **practice my speech/
so I can practice what I preach to the youth**/on the brink of insanity/because 3
strikes poof you gone/**trying to think outside of the box/so many ahks are
locked in**/my pen drops ink so often...*

all bold italics are examples of double/triple entendre.

example 1: is a play on the idea of immaculate conception. I begin the entendre with defying the norm like a virgin birth, then I take the term given to that religious concept and use it to say I conceptually spit immaculate phrases. So the religious meaning of immaculate conception is present in the line, as well as me conceiving immaculate conceptual lyrical phrases.

example 2: chasing dirt, this is a double because we chase dirt in two ways, just about everything that we consume on this planet came from dirt. Our food is grown in the dirt. Our bodies are composed of minerals and materials found in dirt. The clothes we wear, money we have in our pockets, materials used to build our technology comes from the dirt. So we are actually chasing dirt and many of us when we die our bodies will be placed in the dirt. Our material goods that many of us work so hard to get come from the dirt, and for many the final destination of our physical shells will be the dirt.

example 3: practice my speech, I literally practice rhyming but at the same time I practice the message in my words on a daily basis. The next line is a continuation of that. Practice what I preach to the youth. I practice my rhymes so I can deliver them to the youth in a way that will inspire and move them. I also practice the message in my rhymes so the youth can see the reality of the message when they see me.

example 4: think outside of the box so many ahks are locked in, the box can be a cell or a stagnated place of thought. I'm trying to think outside of the pathways that represent institutionalized thinking, and think outside of the stagnated non-revolutionary thought that many of us are stuck in just trying to survive.

6. <u>Homophones</u> - words that sound the same with different meanings.

Example: Moorish Science (Verse 2)

Pre conditioned to spit it/like I was bioengineered with these lyrics/research the genome find it deep in the double helix/mad scientists in the laboratory plotting with chemists/conducting experiments/on how to build the illest of lyricists/hopping up out of that Petrie dish/ on some ill instrumental/reppin that 5th elemental/OnBeats on them periodic turntables rhythm hypnotic/we already got em/you watching, them heads is bobbin/mixing them acids and bases/man, I love how that bass hit/not that base for a basehead/4 balls and a baseman/man, I'm talking about when that bass when it's shaking the basement/the 808 out the speaker that's leaving your face bent/ uh...

I enjoyed writing this wordplay between the words base and bass. They are homophones that depending on context can have a variety of meanings. I was already in a writing scheme that was using science so picking up from acids and bases allowed me to go from the scientific/chemistry concept of a base to the more musical idea of bass. Represented beautifully by the 808 bass drum.

7. Idiom/Colloquialism: a saying, phrase or fixed expression in a culture that has figurative meaning. A word or phrase that is not formal or literary, typically one used in ordinary or familiar conversation.

Example: Time (Fair Grime)

I think of time, minutes, seconds to hours/ days, week, months to years, calendars/ decades, centuries/ we fade into infinity/ time is money/ but for some they say time is an enemy/ man/ Once upon a time/ in a land before time/ where mankind was kind/ and paid attention to the signs/ but then time came/ and man went blind/ searching in vain/ always trying to find time/ but time/ always keep running/ and it never stood still/ one thing man don't understand/ is only time kills/ and there's a time to kill/ but now the time ain't right/ but there's no time left/ So we try to travel through time/ to make it right like Sam Beck/ but we no Marty McFly/ but time flies/ especially if you party waste time with your life/ and destiny is what a man do with his time/ It's time. (This verse is also a good example of repetition. I use the word time in multiple ways throughout the piece)

In this verse I was able to play with idioms and colloquialisms and keep it all in the theme of time.

- This piece is also an example of the literary device **Repetition**.

8. Imagery: the use of words that help create mental images. This is a great way of allowing readers/listeners to visualize the story in their minds.

Example: Praise Be

From a clot of congealed blood, sperm cell to the ovary/
My conception pure poetry/ written before/
Words would ever pour/ from my lips anointed/
my cup runneth over with blessings appointed/
To speak these poignant/ prose on microphones/
Raised where the rose grows through concrete floors/
And natural fo-liage/ locked behind walls of metal and steel cold/
To the touch/ windows to the heaven blocked by soot, smut, fog poisonous smog clogging the lungs of young ones.

God is an emblem which hangs around necks on chain in city slums.
Metallic birds of prey with machine gun talons hover eclipsing the sun
It's chaotic where I'm from Pharaonic numbskulls in power got my bredren dead
men walking to military drum *<u>rolls for crumbs molded over soldiers of misfortune
rolling</u> over in their grave…

I wrote this verse with a lot of visual language in it. I really wanted to paint the
pictures that I was carrying in my mind. I wanted to give the listeners all the
sights, smells, sounds and feels that inspired what made me write.

9. <u>Jargon/Vernacular</u> - language peculiar/specific to a particular trade,
profession, community, culture or group. This is an important concept because in
order for a message to be understood it must be delivered in the language of the
people. I wrote my poems and book in the jargon/vernacular of black people and
other oppressed peoples. They are the people that I wanted my book to reach.
We have been tricked into thinking our jargon/vernacular is not valuable because
of how English speaking white people have used their power to instill supremacy
of their use of Jargon/Vernacular over other usages of English Jargon/
Vernacular.

Example: There is a Devil

…these days can't make heads or tails/cats trying to get they(their) mail/make
bail/chase tail/dreaming of sitting on Spreewells/and changing females/like they
do outfits/when our situation is similar to Auschwitz/big prison and public
housing...

this is a short section from a song entitled There is a Devil, I write it in the
language of the people I come from. We don't always observe the "rules" of
"standardized" English. The "rules" and "standardization" are really a reflection of
preference and power. A segment of the English speaking society preferred
certain spellings and "grammar rules" and they were able to use their power to
force others to accept those rules. I happen to belong to a group of people that
did not voluntarily comes to this land, and didn't choose to learn this language. It
was forced upon my ancestors, so what purpose does a rule have in the
language of your oppressor when you've been stripped of your own language
and now are forced to communicate in their language.

There is nothing wrong with learning the rules of a language and speaking and writing it "correctly" but at the same time there is nothing wrong with communicating in a language in the ways that works best for the group of people you are attempting to address. In the section above I use some slang terms that are popular where I was raised. I use "they" instead of "their" to represent ownership. I know the difference between the two words but at times it's easier to say they instead of their to mean ownership. That's our cultural preference and it makes sense. That's they stuff. Cats trying to get they mail (their money). Chase tale, tale = intimate relationships with a partner. Spreewells = a type of rim on a car tire. Females = is a way some folks refer to women in the street.

10. <u>Juxtaposition</u> - is the overlapping or mixing of opposite or different situations, characters, settings, moods, or points of view in order to clarify meaning, purpose, or perspective.

This is a very useful technique for constructing arguments and making points. I like using story as a way to utilize juxtaposition. At other times I'll present an entire argument or list of points and refute them in a piece using juxtaposition.

One of my earlier pieces that used this concept was entitled Chickens Coming Home to Roost. I wrote this after the Sept. 11, 2001.

Example: Chickens Coming Home to Roost

You wiped out over 100 million indigenous homies/from Iroquois to Ohlone/aztec, Navajo, Seminole, Shoshone/Anasazi/ don't forget the German Nazis they were Christian/now all of this is tied to your nation or your religion/Spanish inquisition, Hiroshima, Nagasaki/I won't omit the crusades and I won't omit the worst form of chattel slavery ever seen in the history of this globe/you got a nerve to call some others a terrorist/the biggest terrorist on the block in fact still be these Americans/ biological warfare testing on their own kind/Tuskeege Experiment/giving black folks syphilis then watch them die/test poisonous pesticides on impoverished farm workers/masters of genocide and apartheid/all of this is a precursor to the destruction of this empire/because we know that what goes up must come down/ but now they fly their flags high yelling semper fi/trying to silence the voices of the past screaming loud in this present day/strange days indeed but you reap what you sew/and they planted hatred and violent seeds/and the deeds of this land will be punished but y'all think you're gonna get off singing God bless

America/when your own founding fore-father Thomas Jefferson said this in fact before he turned to dust/I tremble for this nation when I think that God is just.

The entire piece is a juxtaposition of the narrative the United States and Western Society tries to put out about how great and good it is. I juxtaposed it with a brief history of the atrocities this society is guilty of historically and presently.

11. <u>Metaphor</u> - a comparison between two things that usually are not similar. The comparison is implied rather than directly stated. Key difference between metaphor and simile is that a metaphor does not state the comparison using the words like or as.

Example: Fall In

<u>This life be a tour of duty</u>/but they try to fool me/they feed be bourgeoisie("boujee")/american dreams of jacuzzis/and coogi sweaters/this behooves me/why they slowly take my sector like Israeli Jewish Settlers/ so I keep a fresh pile of rock ready for flying/we can be free then we fin to be dying trying to be/no more iron bars and chains confining me/so we form something stronger than 5 lions/born a soldier like Orion/a walking biological weapon/bio-technology/bionic scholarly device encased in a peasants body...

12. <u>Multi Syllable Rhyme</u> - Creating rhymes with words/phrases based upon multiple parts of the word/phrases rhyming instead of just a common single syllable end rhyme.

Single syllable

Black - Cat (1 syllable)

Multi:

Doctor - Proctor (2 syllable)

Contemplating - Concentrating (4 syllable)

This is one of my favorite writing techniques. It's one thing to make sure that all your lines end with the same rhyme pattern. It's an entirely different practice to write in a way that all syllables in words rhyme.

Example: Tradition (Second Verse)

prepare your mind for expansion/can you fathom/we go from atoms to adam/ design intelligent all because of a pattern/it's intrinsic/they say the wisdom is infinite/and if a tip of a pen is dipped/in oceans with reservoirs that are limitless/to write a manuscript/you still couldn't extinguish it./Feel the rhythm of the algorithmic/this binary mind is balancing the tao and physics/if consciousness is existence/that's postulates possibility is endless/we oscillating between forces tremendous/contemplating source of beginnings/bidiyah nihiyah/alpha omega/we looking for truth is it found in the vedas/Siddartha Guatama found in the shade of/ the Bodhi Tree/and the potency of this poetry/is somewhere on the level of what Oden speaks./Decipher runes in some Roman ruins/on second viewing/Olmec statue nose is looking like it's Patrick Ewing/Tanakh chapters, Qur'an surahs or it's Buddha's Sutras/in a cypher with Shudras/my hand gestures look like Buddha's mudras./They try to knock the hustle they can't knock Nanak the Guru/ they watching Hulu/dud went darkside like Count Duku/I'm making wudu on the steps of pyramid Khufu/holler uhuru/keep on spitting out this black voodoo... (the verse continues with multi syllabic rhymes)

This entire verse was written with multiple syllable rhyme schemes. Almost all patterns are 3 to 4 syllable rhymes. Only a few are 2 syllable rhymes. This is one of my favorite verses for multiple syllable rhymes.

13. <u>Personification</u> - giving human attributes/characteristics to an animal, object or idea.

Example: Umkumto Wa Sizwe (Spear of The Nation)

When my pen taps the paper, <u>the ink begins to dance</u>. <u>It's never choreographed</u>. These are the stories of warriors passed/past. Adrenaline rush, feel the euphoria blast it registers in the pleasure centers of the brain...

In this example the ink in my pen is being personified. I speak of the ink as dancing. This gives the personal characteristic of dance to the ink. Dancing is something people do, so describing the movement of the ink as dancing creates the personification of the ink.

14. <u>Schematic/Thematic Writing</u>: utilizing a conceptual theme to articulate a point. The concept can be based in any type of cultural context.

Example: *Reparations Flow*

There's blood on the street/homie, we Mobb Deep/Witness a prodigy until they martyr me/The mind of a young Carter G./Woodson/Who could pen/A new history Just to show you where the hood been/They still miseducating the negro/ Emasculating our heroes...

There are two themes present in this section. I use the hip hop group Mobb Deep and one of its members Prodigy to illustrate a point. Then that's followed by a historical reference to the genius of Carter G. Woodson and his famous work the Mis-Education of the negro. I use the theme of Mobb Deep to create a scheme of rhyme based on that reference and then do the same with Carter G. Woodson.

- This section also has double entendres.

15. <u>Simile</u> - a comparison between two things that usually are not similar. The comparison is often stated directly using words such as like or as.

Example: Revolutionary Funk (verse 2)

Black fist raised with an afro/like samurai/them boys get on the mic and they pantomime/what it means to be black in this day and time/what i'm spitting be cannon fire/they spitting them candy bars/they stay swearing they hard/ pretending to be a killer/they thinking that make em God/killing they own people/ it's showing them boys is off, showing them boys is lost, showing them boys is lost, showing them boys is gone...

Black fist raised with an afro like Samurai. Here I'm using the anime cartoon character Afro Samurai in a simile. There's a little double entendre here as well. In this song I begin the first verse with a similar opening line. First verse begins: black leather with my brim low/looking like Huey in that window... The second verse takes that same formula to begin but changes the simile and then changes the pacing and pattern of the rhymes that follow.

16. Advanced Alliteration - the repetition of more than just the same beginning letter/sound. What I call advanced alliteration is the repetition of the beginning part of a word, repetition of a prefix or beginning of a word.

Example: Ghetto Messiah (Verse 2)

Born sometime between Vietnam/ and the Iran/ Contra Conflict/ Constant/ Contradiction/ in political mantras/ they confiscate comrades/ call them convicts/ my content controversial/ if you contemplate it/ my ghetto messiah complex is complicated/ from a strong breed concentrated/ in dilapidated environs…

I describe this technique as advanced alliteration, it's the ability to apply basic alliteration but add more to what is being repeated. I bounce between the prefix of con, com contra/contro. You'll find a number of poets and rappers who use variations of this same technique. It is also my belief that poetry and Hip Hop have done so much to advance the ways in which language can be used. We need to create new terminology to define/describe these evolutionary steps in language.

Extra Learning Experiences

Tradition (Verse 1) Tyson Amir

We on mission
Trying to carry on tradition
I know the government listen
They fighting for extradition.
They wishing my right
to the first amendment be rescinded,
because when I'm penning these lyrics
the brothers and sisters in tenements hear it.
They look in the mirror
and start feeling fearless.
They follow me
marching down the block Marcus Garvey appearing
in the flesh
for the second time.
It's red, black and green on the crest
Black Star Line
We been oppressed
because they been obsessed
they been trying to suppress this intellect
since Imhotep the architect,
but we stay building.
I'm on my Benjamin Banneker,
Lewis H. Latimer
giving em light
the reason they mad at us.
They preferring the shadows
while we shining immaculate.
They green with envy
because they can't manufacture it
got the African continent on my amulet.
Feet color of burnt brass
like Jesus of Nazareth.
Every revolution needing a catalyst
from the passages
of The Spook Who Sat By The Door
the protagonist.
I'm moving like I'm Sam Greenlee
in green fatigues
while these Uncle Tom Kermits sipping they green tea.
In these mean streets,
the beast just want to feast,
he just pulled up his seat,
unfolds his handkerchief.
It's like, dinner is served, monsieur bon-appetite.
The judges, the police
the government on the sneak,
the saga never cease,
the cycle on the repeat,
the enemy on the creep
the torch was passed to me.
I'm trying to carry on tradition for my people to be free.
Let's get free!

Black Boy Poems (Cultural Capital) Learning Experience

These questions might seem simple on the surface but they are actually some of the most important questions you'll need to answer in your life. Your answers will be more than just words or thoughts, it will manifest in how you live your life. Think deeply and critically about these answers.

1. Who are you?

_____

_____

_____

_____

2. What is your purpose in light of the experience/history of your people?

_____

_____

_____

_____

3. What do you plan to do with your life in light of the historical and contemporary experience of your people?

_____

_____

_____

_____

Quote responses

Marcus Garvey (What is he saying? What does it mean to you and about you?)

_____

_____

_____

_____

_____

Steve Biko (What is he saying? What does it mean to you and about you?)

_____

_____

_____

_____

_____

George Jackson (What is he saying? What does it mean to you and about you?)

_____

_____

_____

_____

_____

Black Boy Poems Exploratory Learning Experience

Tradition verse 2 (Tyson Amir)

Prepare your mind for expansion
Can you fathom
They say we go from atoms to Adam
Design intelligent all because of a pattern.
It's intrinsic,
they say the wisdom is infinite,
And if a tip of a pen is dipped in oceans with reservoirs that are limitless
to write a manuscript
you still couldn't extinguish it.
Feel the rhythm of the algorithmic.
This binary mind that's balancing the Tao and physics.
If consciousness is existence, that postulates possibility is endless.
We oscillating between forces tremendous.
Contemplating the source of beginnings.
bidiyah nihiyah, alpha omega.
We're looking for truth is it found in the Vedas
or Siddhartha Gautama found in the shade of the Bodhi tree,
And the potency of this poetry is somewhere on the level of what Odin speaks.
Decipher runes in some roman ruins.
On second viewing Olmec statue nose is looking like it's Patrick Ewing.
Tanakh chapters, Quran Surahs or it's Buddhist sutras,
in a cypher with shudras, my hand gestures look like Buddha's mudras.

They try to knock the hustle but can't knock Nanak the Guru.
They off that Hulu.
Dude went dark side like Count Dukoo.
I'm making whudu on the steps of pyramid Khufu.
Holler Uhuru, keep on spitting out this black voodoo.

Traditions we carry be ancient
A myriad of perspectives trying to explain what our place is.
A complicated arrangement of colored faces,
different languages, animals, minerals molecular, matrix
heaven and hell, reincarnation.
They're all sides of the same conversation.
The real question, is it evolution or elevation?
Is it really the fit who survive if the soul and mind are stuck in stagnation?
Hi-technology, but impotent moral interpretations.
We ignore suffering by changing the station
or playing with applications on a smart mobile device.
Thousands in your social network but you can't socialize.
The wolves in sheep clothing are coming, remove the wool from your eyes.
And you reap what you sew, we got a spool full of lies.
Tradition says the way is in the heart, it's not in the sky.
Tradition says the way is in the heart, it's not in the sky.
Tradition says the way is in the heart, it's not in the sky.
And that's the reason why I Carry on tradition.

What feelings/emotions did you experience from reading and listening to the piece?

_____

_____

_____

What thoughts and or questions did it inspire in you? Explain why.

_____

_____

_____

Write down a few examples of tradition/culture that stood out to you in the piece. What made them stand out to you?

_____

_____

_____

Was there a tradition/culture mentioned in the piece that you are connected to? How did it make you feel to see it represented in the piece? How often do you feel your tradition/culture is featured in your learning space? Explain

_____

_____

_____

What does tradition mean to you? What tradition(s) do you feel you carry on? In what ways do you feel your tradition(s) contribute to a more just and equitable society?

_____

_____

_____

_____

Made in the USA
Coppell, TX
26 May 2023

17331267R00162